MW00749235

Lummo

Herb Lummis is affectionately known to his friends as
Lummo.
He is a real knock-around fella who used to be a lot of things:
photographer, horse-breaker and blacksmith.
He was born during World War Two near Bendigo
in North Central Victoria where he still lives.

His father was a farmer and his mother a pianist.
Lummo, the youngest of four children, spent his early life
mainly riding horses and chasing rabbits and foxes.
He also spent many days with a fishing rod in his hand.
He had to learn how to cook because when he and his father
went away they would only take a frypan,
some salt and a bucket of fat and live off the land,
and *Lummo* got tired of eating nothing.

These days he turns a quid by making a range of bush
cooking equipment proudly knocked up out of BHP steel:
open-fire tripods, bush barbecues, fry-pans, bush toasters
plus classic Australian wool-bale hooks.
He also collects and writes bush recipes, bush tales
and country songs. And plays guitar in a country band.
He says he's a pretty ordinary sort of bloke, but his mates say
that after they made *Lummo* they broke the mould.

This publication is dedicated

to my dear old Dad

who passed away a couple of years ago.
To me he was more a mate than a father
and it was this old fella who taught me
how to survive in this wonderful country of ours.

Meet up with you later, Mate.

Rabbit on a Shovel

by

Lummo

Aussies cooking
around the
campfire

REVISED EDITION

This book may be ordered from the publisher,
but try your bookshop first.

Rabbit on a Shovel
PO Box 305
Eaglehawk Victoria 3556
Australia
Call: 03 - 5446 8627

Publisher — Rabbit on a Shovel
In-house Editors — Christine Flynn, Des Carroll

ISBN 0-9751666-0-3.

MANUFACTURED WHOLLY WITHIN AUSTRALIA

CONTENTS

G'day! *Lummo* Welcomes You

As a kid growing up and spending many days at a time in the bush, and of course with no equipment or utensils at all, or if I had them not knowing how to use them, I remember how boring it was to eat fried fish or fried rabbit and rabbit or duck stew day after day. What a change, and how different it would have been, if we had the gear and equipment that is available to us today. And knowing a little bit about cooking would have made life just that much easier.

When I first thought of writing this bush cookbook it was my aim to help some of the people who like to go bush, to give them a few ideas and advice that I have received over the years.

The recipes, advice and directions in this book will help you Bush Cooks improve the standard of dishes you prepare whilst in the bush. If you follow this advice then at least you will have the supplies and the gear needed to serve up a pretty good meal which, with practice, should be as good as you would get at home. Of course how it turns out is completely up to the cook and the cook is only as good as his fire.

I must thank the many people who have helped me make this book possible. The fishermen and cattlemen from the Northern Territory, the shearers' cooks, the mountain men and hunters from the Victorian Alps, the drovers from Central Australia, the fishermen from the mighty Murray River and, of course, the numerous others who spend all their spare time in our precious bush: they have shared their experiences, and were willing to let me use their ideas and advice.

These people have made bush cooking an art, and their recipes which I have included in this cookbook are tried and proven over many campfires. So *Lummo* welcomes you to have a go at bush cooking.

It is my hope that these recipes will be tried and proven over *your* campfire for many years to come.

MILK
LONGLIFE
VEGE
SELF RAISING
FLOUR

Tuckerbox & Gear

NOTICE TO ALL CAMPERS

All you bushies and campers alike
Do us a favour and keep the bush Right
Throw your cans and rubbish in an old plastic bag
You can put it in the boot or use it as a swag
Then take it all home and do the right thing
Chuck it in the house rubbish or in the big green bin.

Lummo's Tuckerbox

Make it yourself. No tradesman's skills required. It is 2' 3" long by 1' 3" high and 1' 3" wide. And it is made out of chipboard.

Ingredients

Chipboard—1/2" is what I use
Some 1" nails
One 6m length of 1" aluminium angle iron
Some 1/2" chipboard screws
Two good hinges
Two good carrying handles
A good quality chest lock

How to do it

First of all, make a complete six-sided box, with no openings, with your glue and nails. Then measure down from the top about 2 inches and cut the lid off as one. This makes for a nice fitting lid. Add two good hinges and screw on. Then paint the box. I paint mine with outdoor fence paint. Cover all the edges with the aluminium angle with screws. Add to each end two carry handles, and add the chest lock to the front to keep it locked and the missus out.

The whole box should cost no more than about $30.00, and is good and solid. I've had mine for a couple of years now and it has seen many a rough trip.

Give it a go. It's easy to do, and they look good.

When you return home after your trip, try to restock your tuckerbox as soon as possible, so that you can be ready for your next time away. Don't forget to keep your box locked so your missus can't get at it when she runs out of provisions in the kitchen.

Tuckerbox Contents

Half a century ago, my dear old mum prepared my first ever tuckerbox. No it wasn't an old spud bag with hay band braces. It was an old soft drink box packed with sugar, salt, sauce, tea , flour, eggs, camp pie, pannikin, plate, knife and fork. As time moved on, the tucker box and it contents increased in size, until the trip around Australia, where it was dramatically reduced.

Here is a list of goodies in my current tuckerbox, when carefully packed contains all the ingredients you need for recipes in this cookbook.

Tucker

125g Salt
50g Pepper
500g Sugar
1kg Plain Flour
1kg Self Raising Flour
500g Cornflour
2 lt Long Life Milk
300g Powdered milk
100 Tea Bags
250g Tea
and Vegetable
200g Instant Coffee
750ml Cooking Oil
500g Dripping
250g Baking Powder
60g Curry Powder
1 tin Gravox
500ml Vinegar
Small jar All Spice

1 Pkt Sultanas
3 Pkts Dried Peas
3 ptks Dried Beans
2 pkt Instant Spud Mix
1 Tin Mushrooms
125g Garlic Granules
600ml Tomato Sauce
250ml Worcestershire Sauce
50ml Tabasco Sauce
Stock cubes Chicken, Beef
250g Lemon concentrate
500g Vegemite
1 tin Golden Syrup
250g Honey
1 jar of Jam
30g Mustard
Small jar Mixed Herbs
1 Small tin cayenne pepper

Gear

***Rabbit on a Shovel* cookbook**
1 carton of matches
1 roll of garbage bags
1 roll Aluminium Foil
Plastic Sealer Bags
1 Scouring Cloth
50ml Detergent
1 grater

4 Pannikins (Large tin mugs)
4 Knifes, Forks and spoons
4 Tin Plates
1 Large Fork
1 can opener
1 egg flip
1 Pkt Skewers

Fresh Tucker

FRESH MEATS

The following fresh meat supplies are only a backup, just in case you can't catch a fish or get a rabbit. It's probably a good idea to keep your fresh meat in an Esky with plenty of ice to keep it from going off.

Steak
Chops
Bacon
Chicken pieces
Sausages
Minced meat

How to choose good meat

The joints should be a nice shape and a bright colour. Mutton is a lighter colour than beef. The meat should not be watery or flabby. The fat should be well mixed in with the lean—if the meat has too much fat it's a waste when cooking, and real lean meat has less value when cooked, so try to get some meat which is between fat and lean.

How to choose a chook

If you're into buying chooks, here are a couple of things to look out for. Young chooks have limp claws, and no spurs on their legs. Chooks with dark coloured legs should be roasted, and the light-feathered variety are ideal for boiling. Don't forget to test the breast bone, it should be sort of pliable, and I love chooks with plump breasts.

What about a turkey

Well, what about it? It's eyes should be full and bright. Its feet and legs smooth and black, and with short spurs.

FRESH FISH

This is for the blokes who have been away all weekend and played up like hell and didn't catch anything for obvious reasons. So on the way home bought some fish from the local pub.

How to choose a good healthy fish

The gills must be red. The flesh has to be firm. The eyes should be clear, full and bright. The scales should be intact. It should smell alright. The smaller fish are usually better.

FRESH FRUIT AND VEGIES

Either at home or away everybody needs their vegies, even the old-timers used to eat their yams and berries.

Bananas	**Tomatoes**	**Carrots**
Apples	**Potatoes**	**Onions**

How to handle fresh vegies

Fresh vegies, as you know, are perfect with all dishes you bash up at home or in the bush. But there are a couple of rules to follow. Always use them as quickly as possible. If refrigeration is a problem, try to keep them in a cool dark airy place. Wash them properly, boil them quickly with the lid on, and strain them as soon as they are tender. Don't forget to use the vegetable water for making sauces and gravy.

FRESH PROVISIONS

These fresh provisions will certainly help add variety to your main dishes and should last a fair time without refrigeration.

Bread	**Cheese**	**Crumpets**
Margarine	**Eggs**	

Bits And Pieces You May Need

UTENSILS

When you're away from home, you need a few comforts. Here are certain pieces of equipment which are fairly important and others which are well-and-truly needed.

Shovel
Axe
Chainsaw
Rabbit traps
Hooks
Lengths of chain
Water bucket
Steel tripods
Fire stakes *or*
Star pickets
Jaffle iron
Grill
Camp oven
Bush frypans
Billy
Saucepan
Toasting fork
Cake Tin

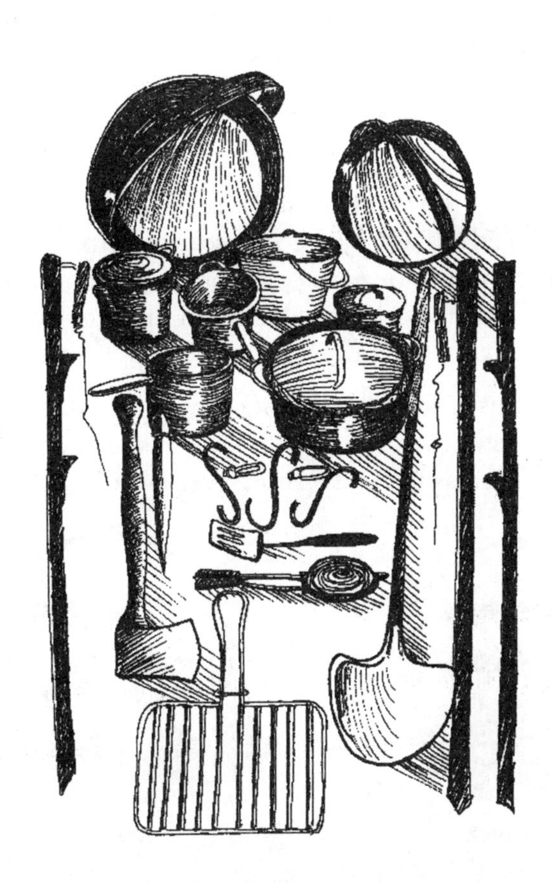

Camp Ovens

There are two kinds of camp ovens. The first kind is made from thick heavy cast iron and the second from 2 mm spun steel.

Cast-iron ovens are sometimes called *Dutch Ovens*. The most famous Australian cast-iron oven is called a *Furphy*, and is made by the family-owned Furphy foundry in Shepparton, Victoria. This foundry also achieved fame with its *Furphy* water carrier which accompanied our soldiers to the Middle East during the First World War. The *Furphy* water carrier was hauled from camp to camp by horse-drawn carts, the drivers of which were renowned for the gossip they carried along with the water. And this is how we got the Australian saying: *a bit of a furphy*, meaning rumour or false report.

The steel oven is called a *Bedourie* oven, and was invented by some stockmen in the south-west Queensland town of Bedourie. The advantage of the *Bedourie* over the *Furphy* was that you could put the *Bedourie* on a packhorse and if the horse bucked and threw its pack, the steel oven didn't break like the old brittle cast-iron pots did.

Both ovens are used interchangeably these days, although some cooks would prefer that the *Bedourie* was made of 3 mm rather than 2 mm steel so as to hold a more even heat.

FURPHY

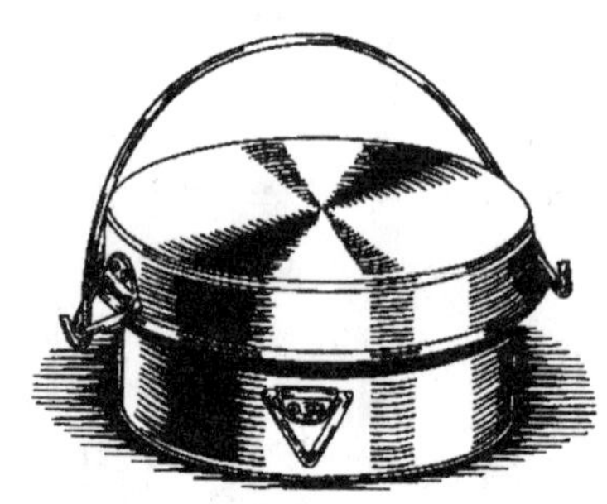

BEDOURIE

Davo's Dunny

Everybody has to go at some stage, and this dunny is a beauty. It doesn't cost much, is easy to make, takes up no room and is portable. Everybody who goes bush should have one.

Ingredients

3/4" chipboard 500 × 500 mm

4 × 100 mm lengths of 33 mm (outside diameter) square steel tube

4 × 500 mm lengths of 25 mm (outside diameter) square steel tube

4 × 40 mm × 3 mm × 100 mm long flat steel bars

8 × 18 mm × 25 mm nuts & bolts

4 × star steel pickets

Some canvas

How to do it

Take the chipboard and round off the outside corners. With your jigsaw cut a hole in the middle about the same size as the pan seat in your house toilet.

Cut one end of each of your 33 mm square steel tubes at 60 degrees and weld onto the middle of the 40 mm face of the flat steel bars. Drill 2 holes (18 mm) in each end of each flat steel bar and bolt to seat equal distances apart.

Fit your smaller (25 mm) removable square steel tubes, as removable legs. Paint to weatherproof.

How to use it

Dig a hole in the ground approximately 18 inches deep and place portable dunny above. Belt in 4 star pickets and affix some canvas around.

Then use as required.

When leaving your campsite, don't forget to fill in the hole.

Family Jewels Purse

If you ever happen to run into, or find a freshly-dispatched big red 'Roo, and you wish to make up with your missus for all the camping trips you've made in the past, why not make her a little gift? Interested? Well read on.

Ingredients

One big red 'Roo
1 bootlace
A stick (about 1" thick)
1 billy of tea-leaves & sludge
Handful of cooking salt
1 yonnie or stone (about 3" across)

How to do it

When skinning off your 'Roo's scrotum, include a 4-inch diameter of belly skin.

When the scrotum has been completely removed turn it inside out and place a good round yonnie, or throwing stone, inside the hair part of the bag. Place the piece of wood through the opening and down to the stone.

Allow it to dry quietly in a suspended ventilated spot, with a piece of string tied outside of the bag and around the top of the wood. Rub in a good handful of cooking salt before drying. When dry, remove all fat from the skin and remove stone.

Tanning can commence. Tanning can be done several ways. Here is a favourite way. Gather all your tea-leaves and sludge and place into a billy. Place the skin in the billy and leave for 3 weeks, stirring up at least once a day.

Remove skin from the billy and dry slowly, constantly rubbing to make skin soft. Carefully cut slots into skin where the string has been tied. Place a bootlace into the slots, in and out to make a drawstring, and reverse the hair to the outside. By this time it should be lovely and soft and pliable.

I tell you what—when you give this purse to your lady to put her small change in she will be as pleased as punch. If she doesn't like it, keep it for yourself, because it will be one of the best tobacco pouches this side of Myers Creek.

Twelve Gallon Oven

My old dad who was born at the turn of the century used to use this type of oven to cook in, especially when we went up to the river. We believe it originated in Northern Australia but even now a lot of the old-timers are still using them and cooking up really good meals. Why not try one, just for the fun of it?

Ingredients

12 gallon drum (empty) with the top cut out
A bit of flat tin or plate for a shelf
A bit of flat tin or plate (hinged if you want) for a door
4 legs (if you're serious)

How to do it

Get your drum and cut the top right out.

Lay the drum on its side. Get a bit of flat plate for shelf to cook on. The shelf should be positioned about half-way up the drum. On the top of your drum (which is lying on its side) punch half a dozen or so holes, to let out the smoke.

If you are real serious about your oven, as my dad was, you can weld four legs onto it as a stand. You can also hinge a flat piece of steel onto the front for a door, or you can just lean a piece of steel over the front opening—either way works good.

Now that you have done all this, it is *important* before using your drum to cook in, to make sure you give it a good burn out first, to get rid of all the oil and rubbish.

Shove in your cake or scones or your *Twelve Gallon Bun*, and shut the door and let nature do its work.

But Can You Boil That Billy?

Bush cleaner

Your forks and spoons in your tuckerbox look dull. Well, get a bucket and chuck in some water and a handful of salt and a bit of tin foil rolled into a ball. Put in the forks and spoons and leave them there for about an hour. Wipe clean.

Cooking With Coals

As a young bloke I enjoyed going bush with my dad. To me he was a master bushman, survivor and a good teacher of life, he was always the boss. He would say to me, "when we get there, the first thing we gotta do, get the fire going."

It didn't matter if we were in the mallee or heading north he would have no trouble getting a fire started because of the nature of the wood. It was a different if we went south or to the mountains, the wood in those areas was always damp therefore more difficult to start. His fire was the most important part of his survival, he would spend a lot of time and energy making sure the fire was perfect for his next meal. He said to me on many occasions, "Got a lousy fire got lousy tucker".

He would start his fire with plenty of good wood; he always had lots of wood on hand, mainly stumps. He would dig a cooking hole away from the main fire and start laying a bed of coals from the main fire to the cooking fire; he kept feeding both fires until he was ready to start cooking his tea.

If he was cooking with the camp oven, his new bed of coals was perfect for the job with a nice shovelful of coals on the lid. If he was cooking with the shovel or the hot plate he would use the same coal fire for its even heat. He would keep the main fire burning for warmth and to keep his water supply hot, as well as for more coals to cook over.

The good old jaffle iron works best when used in the coals, the old trusty 12-gallon oven cooks best with coals put in the lower part of the drum; the art of making good toast is in front of a good bed of hot coals.

Do yourself a favour put some effort into your fire and you will be rewarded with some good results and if the meal is lousy, don't blame the fire.

Basic Cooking

You're probably a good fisherman, shooter, footballer, cricketer and lover. But can you cook? You said No!! Well read on. Here are a few basic recipes you can learn, either in the bush or at home.

BOILED SPUDS

Ingredients

1 good-sized spud for each person
Some salt
Water

How to do it

Peel and rinse the spud and cut into small pieces. Put into a saucepan and cover with water, if required add a pinch of salt. Put saucepan with lid on over a medium heat until water boils, then simmer until cooked. Check by pushing a fork easily into a spud piece.

TO MASH: Tip out water, add a dash of milk, a good dob of margarine or cream, a dash of pepper. Mash the lot with a fork or a masher until nice and smooth. Then serve.

FRIED SNAGS

Ingredients

3 or 4 snags for each person
A little margarine

How to do it

Get your frypan nice and warm-to-hot. Put a little margarine in to melt, pop in the snags, turning often to make sure of even cooking. When nice and brown on the outside, check inside by cutting—when colour is light brown they're done.

SOFT-BOILED EGGS

Ingredients

1 egg for each person
Water

How to do it

Half fill a medium-sized saucepan with water and let boil. Reduce to simmer, then pop the eggs in, shell and all. Check your watch. Let simmer for 3 minutes then remove and use.

TO HARD-BOIL EGGS: Simmer for 10 minutes.

EGGSHELL CRACKED

When hard-boiling an egg, if the shell cracks put a small pinch of salt to the crack, this will help to stop the shell from cracking any further, but if it does, throw it away and get another egg.

To Boil That Billy

Whenever we get our campfire going out in the bush I am constantly being asked how to make the fire stakes which I use, and which over the years have helped to cook many a good meal and boil many a good brew of billy tea.

How to do it

There are many ways of holding that billy or frypan over the campfire. Here are a few ideas:

FIRE STAKES

You need two star pickets with two lugs welded on them at the top. They are driven into the ground, with another star picket resting across the top and sitting in the lugs. Then you need a couple of lengths of chain to hold frypans or billies.

Another way is to have just the two star pickets with a further star picket resting across the top in the slot provided.

STEEL TRIPOD

There are several other ways of holding that billy and the most popular is the steel tripod. These can be either made or bought, and come in various different heights and weights, depending on your needs.

COLLAR AND ARM

Another popular holding device is the collar and arm. It is usually a star picket with a steel collar and a swinging arm.

Whatever device you use, make sure it is strong and dependable, so that it won't collapse and spill your tea or cause a serious burn.

Making Billy Tea

Old timers and swaggies in particular were masters at making billy tea. There are many different ways and methods of doing this; all they wanted to do is to make a real good brew of tea.

How to do it

Start by putting some water in a billy with a wire handle, suspend it over a camp fire, bring it to the boil and add a handful of tea leaves. We are now on our way to making a perfect brew.

Next, we have to try and force the tea leaves to the bottom of the billy so they can draw. There are several ways of doing this.

One way is to tap the billy on the side with a stick. Another way, and the most popular is "the windmill action". This action is one you can use if you want to impress your mates. The plan is, to grab the billy by the handle while the tea is boiling inside, swing it in a big circle from your knees to above your head at high speed, while keeping your elbow straight.

The real fair dinkum billy tea is greatly improved by adding some fresh gum leaves to the billy before pouring. Another way is to stir your tea with a nice fresh green gum stick.

There is nothing more tranquil than sitting on a stump under an old gum tree in front of a roaring camp fire sipping a pannikin of freshly made billy tea.

DIRTY SOAP

To stop soap getting dirty while out in the bush, cut the leg out of your wife's pantyhose and tie the soap in the toe end. Hang the leg of the panty hose in a tree near your wash-up area.

Have A Go At These If You're Desperate

PIZZA
WE DELIVER
ANYWHERE

Three Blokes & a Ute

In the spring of 1963, three desperado's, "Longin , Father and Lummo" loaded up the old EK Ute, we had a sleeping bag each, a tarp, some water, a small tucker box and the trusty camp oven, we headed for Western Australia to have a look at some property.

At Port Augusta, Longin said "why don't we turn right here and go via Darwin?" What a trip. Dust, dirt and potholes all the way to Alice. We turned left and headed to Ayres Rock; not much there, only a couple of shacks and a bloke riding a horse, so we continued on to Darwin, then down the west coast, still all dirt roads. We found Perth, then found the property and immediately drove towards home. Then the dreaded Nullarbor, more dust, dirt and potholes. We were knackered and the Ute was stuffed. The tucker box was nearly empty and we were out of water. When we stopped near the S.A. border, we made a decision to cook what we had, and the next day to make a run for the bitumen to replenish our supplies and try and fix the Ute.

This is all the food we had left, when your tired, hungry and desperate you will eat just about anything, we would have given our right arm and our left leg for a pizza.

Ingredients

1 cooked rabbit
1 opened can of baked beans
1 small can of beetroot
2 small cooked goat chops
Half can of camp pie
Half a dozen cans of hot beer

The way Father did it

He got a fire going, and then hung the camp oven over it. Gathered up the rabbit and goat chops, threw them in the hot camp oven, tipped in the baked beans, the camp pie and beetroot, then added a couple of cans of beer and let it simmer for a while. Then yelled, "Tuckers on." Fair dinkum, this crap tasted sensational, but I'd hate to try and live on it.

P.S.: We got home 6 days later, had travelled over 12,000 miles; 8,000 miles of that were on dirt roads in 5 weeks.

Desperado S'getti

This is the tucker for the desperate man, and its best attribute is that it will be hot and will fill that empty spot.

Ingredients

1 can of spaghetti
4 slices of cheese
4 slices of bread
1 medium chopped onion
1 dob of margarine
1 small spoon of curry powder

How to do it

In a saucepan or frypan brown the chopped onion, tip in the can of spaghetti and stir until nearly done.

In the meantime cook your 4 pieces of toast and have them ready on your plate. When your spaghetti is nice and hot stir in the curry powder. Put the cheese slices on the buttered toast and pour the spaghetti over.

Then wash down with a cuppa tea.

Dogs havin' a go at the rubbish

Simply splash some kero on the bin or bag, or squirt it with some fly spray. They hate it.

Hair Of The Dog

Bit off colour eh? Rough night, must have been something in the tucker, or perhaps the sleep didn't help. Ah well, this will help pick you up.

Ingredients

1 egg
Small spoon of sugar
1 pannikin of milk
Dash of brandy (if available)

How to do it

Beat the egg well, then add milk and sugar and stir thoroughly in a pannikin. Add a touch of brandy if you can handle it.

It's a bit hard to put down but hold your nose, close your eyes, count to ten, then sip slowly. It can't make you feel any worse than you do now.

Jackass Flaps

That's the name the old-timers used to call these things, but we call them bush doughnuts. They don't look much but they're worth a go.

Ingredients

A couple of slices of bread per person
Enough margarine and jam to spread
1/2 pannikin of milk
1 pannikin of self-raising flour
A couple of eggs
A pinch of salt
1/2 pannikin of sugar
Some margarine

How to do it

Stir eggs, milk and sugar in a bowl. Slowly add the flour while mixing, then add salt and mix into a smooth batter.

Dip your jam sandwich into the batter making sure it is completely covered. Drop into a hot pan with some margarine and cook until golden brown on both sides.

'Ungry Beans

The meal for the hungry ones, especially if you have just arrived at your campsite.

Ingredients

1 can of baked beans
1 onion
2 or 3 rashers of bacon
1 dob of Vegemite

How to do it

Dice the bacon and onion, then lightly brown. Open a can of beans and tip into saucepan with the onions and bacon and heat. When warm add a dollop of Vegemite and stir well.

When hot, serve on thick toast with plenty of margarine.

Welsh Rabbit

If the rabbits have been lucky and won the day, here's a way to eat rabbit without a rabbit—Welsh Rabbit.

Ingredients

1 slice of bread
1 teaspoon of jam
1 slice of cheese
1/2 teaspoon of Worcestershire sauce
1/2 teaspoon tomato sauce

How to do it

Mix the jam and sauces together, spread on top of the bread and cover with a cheese slice. Place in greased camp oven and cook until bread is brown and cheese is melted.

Serve hot as an ideal light snack.

Damper & Dough Staples

Aussie Damper

Be a real Aussie, put on your Akubra and moleskins and sing Waltzing Matilda while making this simple version of the Aussie damper.

Ingredients

6 pannikins of self-raising flour
1 spoonful of salt
3 good spoonfuls of margarine
1 pannikin of milk or water

How to do it

In a dish mix the flour and salt together. Then add the margarine and rub together with your fingers until the flour mixture becomes a course texture. Gradually add the milk and water and mix until a stiff dough forms, you can add a little more flour or water if need be. Cover the dough with foil and put to one side for 15 minutes. Prepare the camp oven by rubbing the sides and bottom with flour. Place the prepared dough in the camp oven and place the oven into the coals of your cooking fire, don't forget to put some coals on the lid.

Cooking time should be about 30 minutes, give it a bit of a tap on top if it sounds hollow and its golden brown it's done.

When you take the damper out of the camp oven and smother it with margarine, there is no better tasting food in Australia than Aussie damper cooked in the coals.

Fried Damper

This is delicious cooked up in your warm camp oven after making Meat Loaf for tonight's tea.

Ingredients

1 pannikin of self-raising flour
Pinch of salt
1 egg
Some milk

How to do it

Place flour and salt in a bowl, break egg into centre of flour and mix well. Add milk to make a nice smooth batter.

When Meat Loaf is cooked, remove from camp oven and keep warm. Remove most of the fat and re-heat in camp oven until the remaining fat is bubbling. Pour in the damper mixture, replace lid on camp oven and cook for 20 minutes.

When cooked serve with *MEAT LOAF* and with roast spuds. Have a delicious meal.

Lead Sinkers

These dumplings are the perfect addition to any stew. Or they can be cooked with GOLDEN SYRUP SAUCE and eaten as dessert.

Ingredients

1 pannikin of self-raising flour
2 pinches of salt
1 good spoonful of margarine
Water

How to do it

Knead margarine into flour and salt, mix with enough water to make a stiff dough. Roll into balls.

These dumplings can now be added to your stew, or *GOLDEN SYRUP SAUCE*, and cooked for about 10 minutes.

Quick Damper

I was up the river recently and camped in a real good spot not far from a bloke and his missus who were camped in a caravan. And on the second night I went over to say G'day and the bloke was cooking up this damper. I told him what I was about and he told me his recipe for the damper he was cooking. I asked him where he got it and he told me his father gave it to him as a boy.

Ingredients

3 pannikins of self-raising flour
1 good spoon of powdered milk
Some salt, not too much
Some water

How to do it

Mix all the dry bits together and then mix with the water until you get a good stiff dough. Grease your camp oven and put it in the coals until it's hot. Put your dough in and cook until it's golden brown. Don't forget to put some coals onto the lid of the camp oven.

Cooking should take about half an hour, but keep checking on it by tapping or pushing a knife into the damper.

When it's done, it's time to smother it with margarine and clean up the gravy from the stew.

Bush broom

The old bushman's favourite. Tie some small green branches onto a main handle, then trim off the ends for a perfect bush broom.

Glennasticks

We were camping out of Deniliquin and a lady was doing the cooking and her husband said, "Hey love, what about some Glennasticks?" I said, "What the hell are they?" And he said, "These are her favourite way to cook damper mix." I said "OK". Her name was Glen, and her husband calls 'em Glennasticks.

Ingredients

Quick Damper mix (see recipe)
A green stick
Some margarine
Some jam

How to do it

Get a green stick about 1/2 inch across and about 2 foot long off a tree.

Roll out the damper mix into a strip, say about 9 inches long and about 1 inch wide by nearly 1/2 inch thick. Wind around the end of the stick, "similar to putting electrical tape on the bare wires on your trailer pull".

When you've done this, hold the damper over the coals and keep turning until cooked. When it's cooked pull the stick out—should come out pretty easy.

Fill the centre of the damper with margarine and then stuff in as much jam as you can and hop into it.

Dessie's Scones

For a change of diet, and if you're sick of damper or commercial bread, why not give these pan-fried scones a go? They are delicious and easy to knock up.

Ingredients

2 pannikins of self-raising flour
A couple of pinches of salt
1/2 spoonful of sugar
Milk
Some cheese

How to do it

Mix flour, salt, sugar and grated cheese to taste. Gradually add milk, mixing to make a soft dough. Roll out flat with a beer bottle (about 1/2 inch thick). Cut into squares.

Have your pan warm, sprinkle with flour, add the scone pieces and cook on one side, then turn and cook over a low heat until the scones are firm inside.

Perfect for slopping up stew juices.

Edward River Scones

About 120 years ago, old Jack, a boundary rider and fencing contractor, moved with his wife and family to a station far north of Deniliquin. Jack being a typical colonial bushie would be away from home for months on end, leaving his wife Annie with minimal provision, little money, and nowhere to spend it. Annie's means of survival for herself and the kids was her ingenuity with the limited provisions available, and part of their staple diet was the basic scone. This is her Edward River Scone.

Ingredients

2 pannikins of flour
1/2 teaspoon of salt
1 spoonful of margarine
3/4 pannikin of milk

How to do it

Rub margarine into flour and salt with your fingertips until the mixture resembles breadcrumbs. Quickly mix in sufficient milk to make a soft dough. Turn onto a floured board or cardboard box and knead lightly until smooth. Roll out to 3/4 inch thick. Cut into squares, or into rounds with a floured pannikin, and bake in a hot camp oven.

Variations

Cheese scones—before adding milk add 1/2 pannikin of grated cheese.

Farmhouse Scones

If the missus won't cook you any scones or anything like that, well there is only one thing to do, do it yourself and this is an easy way of doing it.

Ingredients

1 1/2 pannikins of self-raising flour
A good pinch of salt
Good spoon of margarine
1/2 pannikin of milk

Filling mixture

4 rashers chopped bacon
1 grated onion
3/4 pannikin of grated cheese

How to do it

Rub margarine into flour and salt, add milk to make a stiff dough. If dry add more milk.

Roll mixture out flat, say 2/3 inch thick. Spread with filling of chopped bacon, grated onion, and grated cheese. Roll up and cut roll into 1-inch-wide strips. Put into a hot greased camp oven and cook for 20 minutes.

Ideal side-dish or snack. Bloody!!!!! lovely.

Johnny Cake

There are several ways of cooking Johnny Cakes. In the early days the recipe depended on which area you came from. This particular recipe comes from Central Victoria and was given to me by an old-timer who is now in his 90s. He tells me that his grandfather used Johnny Cakes as part of his staple diet. This is how he cooked them.

Ingredients

A couple of pannikins of flour
A good pinch of salt
Some milk or water
A dob of margarine

How to do it

In a container, mix the milk or water with the flour and some salt to make a soft dough mixture. Turn onto a floured board or cardboard box and knead lightly until nice and smooth. Roll out to about 1 inch thick.

Grease the hot frypan with the margarine and lay the complete cake into the bottom of the pan. If you want it brown on both sides, carefully turn the cake over when nearly cooked.

When ready, cover with margarine. Eat with some stew, rabbits or fish.

Lummo's Yam Rocks

While you're down fishing get the missus to bash up a set of these potato scones for a mid-afternoon snack. They are great.

Ingredients

1/2 pannikin of milk
1/4 pannikin of water
3/4 pannikin of instant potato flakes
1 pannikin of self-raising flour
1 pinch of salt
1 egg
1 teaspoon of baking powder

How to do it

Heat (do not boil) the milk and water in a saucepan. Add potato flakes and mix gently. Spoon potato mix into an ice-cream container and sift flour over potato, add baking powder and a pinch of salt. Mix all together with a beaten egg to form a fairly firm dough.

Turn dough onto a floured board or cardboard box and turn several times from the outside in. Roll out to 3/4 inch thickness and cut into sections.

Place scones into a very hot greased camp oven and bake for 15–20 minutes.

Puftaloons

Try this for a different taste.

Ingredients

Aussie Damper mixture (see recipe page 31)

How to do it

Hang the pan over the coals and heat. Then chuck in a liberal amount of margarine. Break the damper mixture into small lumps and pat flat and fry in the frypan.

They don't take too long, and I reckon you'll enjoy 'em, especially with some *Scrub Relish*.

Tying the load to the ute

If tying something extra tight is the job at hand, you need the extra strength of the truckies' hitch. There are many different ways of tying this hitch but if you tie it similar to half a sheepshank you are on the right track. Don't forget to tie back the loops as a guarantee not to slip. Tie the loose ends with a clove hitch.

Truckies' Hitch

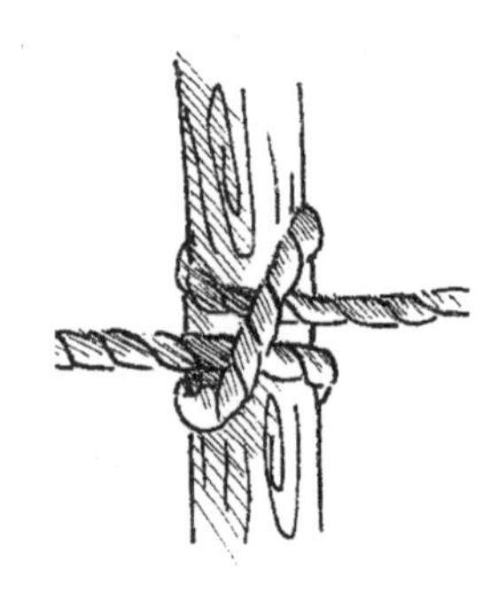

Clove Hitch

Unreal Fillings

OK, so you're off fishin', remembered everything—water bag full, bait, fishin' rod, fuel for the boat, don't forget fuel for yourself. Pile these fillings between damper, bread or scones and "be happy".

CHEESE & ONION

Ingredients

1 chopped onion
1/2 pannikin of grated cheese
1/2 little spoon of mustard
2 eggs
Salt and pepper
A little milk

How to do it

Brown the onions, add rest of the ingredients to frypan and stir until cheese is melted and eggs are cooked. If too thick add a little more milk.

CHICKEN ON THE WING

Ingredients

A big dob of margarine
1 grated onion
1 heaped spoon of grated cheese
1 medium tomato—skinned
1 egg—beaten
Salt and pepper

How to do it

Put all ingredients except the egg into a pot and simmer gently until the onion is cooked. Add beaten egg and simmer until thick.

RED AND YELLOW

Ingredients

4 rashers of bacon
2 eggs
Salt and pepper

How to do it

Chop bacon into fine pieces and fry. When nearly cooked add eggs, salt and pepper and stir until cooked.

TURKEY GOBBLE

Ingredients

A big dob of margarine
A good lump of cheese—chopped
1/2 pannikin of breadcrumbs
Salt, pepper and mixed herbs to taste
1 ripe tomato
1 slice of onion
1 egg—beaten

How to do it

Skin and cut up tomato, chop onion, and cook in a saucepan with margarine until tender. Add cheese and cook for 5 minutes. Add breadcrumbs and a beaten egg and cook again. Add mixed herbs and salt and pepper to taste. Unreal tucker.

Soups To Sit Back And Sip On

Billy Beef Tea

This is second-best only to genuine billy tea. Easy to do, and the Sheilas like it as well.

Ingredients

1/2 lb of shin beef, or gravy beef, or something
1/2 pannikin of water
A few drops of lemon juice
Some salt, not too much

How to do it

Put the water, lemon and salt into a pot. Shred the meat, across the grain, and soak it in the pot for 20 minutes or so. Put the pot over the fire until the meat turns a little brown. Keep stirring all the time.

Now listen: don't let it boil or you will stuff it up.

When that's done, pour out the liquid and sit back and sip it quietly, while munching on a *JOHNNY CAKE* or something.

Myers Creek Moosh

There's nothing better than a big bowl of vegie soup, and the good thing about it is that if you make enough you can have a couple of goes at it.

Ingredients

A big dollop of margarine
2 carrots
2 onions
2 potatoes
2 good spoons of flour
4 pannikins of water
2 beef stock cubes

How to do it

Get your camp oven hot and melt in the margarine. Chuck in the chopped-up vegies but don't brown. Sprinkle flour over and cook until nearly done. Add water and stock cubes and cook for another 30 minutes or so.

The ideal way to eat this Moosh is with some damper or scones.

Cutting a bottle

Find a clear bottle and fill to a point where you wish to break the bottle off. Tie a piece of grease- or petrol-soaked string around the water mark and set fire to the string. The bottle should break off along the burnt line. Use as a carrying vessel or a candle holder.

'Roo Tail Soup

For when you've been out all day and you've worked like a slave. Your belly is rumbling—all you need is a feed. You cooked him this morning, and oh boy, you will see that old 'Roo Tail Soup just bubbling in steel.

Ingredients

One 'Roo tail
Some flour
Water
Bit of pepper and some salt
Big dob of margarine
A couple of diced bacon rashers
A couple of chopped spuds
A chopped carrot, if any
A diced onion

How to do it

Have your camp oven hot. Remove the hairs off the tail and cut into lengths of a couple of inches. Bake the tail pieces for about 2 hours.

Remove the skin, which should come off easily. Coat the pieces with some flour, and put into a pot with enough water to cover. Add the spuds, onions, bacon, carrot, margarine, salt and pepper. Let simmer gently for 90 minutes or so, until the meat hops off the bone—then she's done.

The only way to serve this top soup is with a genuine *AUSSIE DAMPER*. Just ask any old Aussie swaggie.

Supa Beaut Vegemite Soup

It's black, it's hot, looks 'orrible, tastes great, and after all if you're hungry it's better than eatin' nothin'.

Ingredients

1 big spoonful of Vegemite
Boiling water
Bread
Big dob of margarine

How to do it

In a soup bowl mix the Vegemite, margarine and boiling water until all is dissolved. Break a couple of bits of bread into the soup and hop into it.

They feed it to little kids and the oldies so it must be alright.

GOT THE HICCUPS

Stick your middle index fingers behind your earlobes and press, not too hard, and hold for about a minute or so. This'll stop 'em. If not, have another can.

Eggs To Bet On

Aussie Omelette

A meal with the lot. But if your tuckerbox is down a little on content, you can make this very tasty omelette with only cheese and onion. All you have to do is follow the recipe.

Ingredients

3 eggs
1 good pinch of salt
1 good pinch of pepper
1 small sliced spud
1 rasher of bacon
1 small chopped onion
2 slices of cheese
1 tomato
1 spoonful of margarine
1/4 cup of milk

How to do it

Heat pan, melt margarine, add chopped onions, bacon and potatoes. When cooked, slice tomato and place in pan. Beat eggs, salt, pepper and milk together and pour over top of other ingredients. Add cheese.

When set, fold in half and cook a little longer. Serve.

Birds' Nests

For breakfast, dinner or tea, these Birds' Nests will make any bushman's mouth water.

Ingredients

A double handful of spuds
1 spoonful of margarine
Some milk
Salt and pepper
4 eggs
4 or 5 slices of cheese, chopped finely or grated

How to do it

Boil spuds, tip water out, add margarine and milk and mash until smooth. Shape the mashed potato into 4 nest-type dishes and put these into the greased hot camp oven.

Break an egg into each nest. Sprinkle salt, pepper and cheese on top. Bake until eggs are set.

Serve with *Aussie Damper* or *Bushies' Fried Scones.*

SCRAMBLED EGGS GONE MUSHY

You cooked them too quick. Get some of the liquid out. Then chuck in a good lump of margarine or butter and beat well.

Chook In Scrambled Eggs

There's no better way to start the day off, especially in the bush, than after a quick check of the fishing lines to tuck into a good old-fashioned feed of scrambled eggs.

Ingredients

3 eggs (per person)
1 chicken stock cube
1 pinch of salt
1 spoonful of margarine
1 pinch of pepper
1/4 pannikin of milk

How to do it

Beat eggs and milk together with salt and pepper. Hang pan over coals to heat. Grease with margarine. Pour mixture into hot pan, add crumbled chicken cube and stir constantly until cooked. Serve on fresh damper dripping with margarine.

Fried Bread

This is the modern version of "dripping smothered bread" which was cooked on the top of the old wood stove.

Ingredients

2 eggs
Some milk
Bread slice
Salt and pepper
Margarine

How to do it

Warm the fry pan or bush barbie, melt in a dollop of margarine. Mix the eggs with some milk, salt and pepper, dip the bread into the mixture and place into the hot pan. Let it fry for a couple of minutes then turn. When golden brown its done.

Serve with a dash or two of tomato sauce.

Red Chooks

If you like eggs and bacon, well you'll love this. It's ideal on arriving at the campsite. Get the fire going, open a can and put the pan on.

Ingredients

4 eggs
2 rashers of bacon
4 good-size tomatoes
Salt and pepper
Margarine
Breadcrumbs

How to do it

Cut the top off the tomatoes and scoop out the pulp. Dice the bacon and partly cook, then put into the bottom of the tomatoes together with some breadcrumbs and some tomato pulp. Break an egg into each tomato on top of the bacon and breadcrumbs, and give the eggs a bit of salt and pepper. Put into a camp oven, but not too hot, and cook until the eggs are set. Serve hot with damper dripping with margarine.

Red Sunrise

A quick-and-easy breakfast or the ideal brunch, especially if you've had a hard night before.

Ingredients

4 or 5 eggs
2 onions, diced
Salt and pepper
3 or 4 rashers of bacon, chopped finely
1 tin of tomatoes or 4 medium fresh ones

How to do it

Brown the onions and bacon in the pan, then add sliced or tinned tomatoes. When the tomatoes are simmering, break eggs into mixture. Cover with a lid for a few minutes until the eggs have set, then mix the eggs in with the rest with a fork. Serve on hot buttered toast.

Your Rabbit — Cooking Him Up

Rabbit On A Shovel — Song

by *Lummo*

You've had enough for the day, didn't catch a fish, missed out on the rabbits, there're ants in your tuckerbox, and the missus won't cook you any tea! In other words things are rotten. Well have a go at this little song, and if you're musically inclined the key is D. Big deal.

There's a rabbit cooking on a shovel
What a hearty meal
There's a rabbit cooking on a shovel
What a hearty meal
Just throw some spuds and onions in
The taste is so unreal
There's a rabbit cooking on a shovel
What a hearty meal

The boys went out to the bush one day
To get the evening grub
The rabbit he's not hard to catch
He kept them on the run
They searched and searched and searched for him
But they were out of luck
Say Fellas where're all the rabbits
"Cookin' on a shovel"

Repeat first verse

If the rabbits are scarce and you're hungry too
Well take a note of this
Why not go to the river and try to catch some fish
If the fish don't bite and you're out of luck
I know just how you feel
Try some damper from our cookbook man
Or perhaps an Achilles Eel

Repeat first verse twice.

The Rabbit

As we already know, the rabbit was introduced to Australia compliments of our early pioneers from England, and has increased in numbers over the years to such an extent that it is in plague proportions in some areas of this country.

Due to its availability in most parts of Australia, and as it is such an easy catch, the good old rabbit is one of the most popular pieces of meat to be cooked over our campfires.

In the early days when the barbie plate wasn't around, most folk would use the shovel. A simple tool that was always carried, it would dig rubbish holes, fire pits and drains around the camp. After being cleaned up a bit, it served as a frypan as well—but watch out, as this takes the temper out of the shovel's blade.

My dear old mate Roy, who worked in the Victorian Alps many years ago, told me of the many times they would have A RABBIT ON A SHOVEL for tea. They had to, as most times they had nothing else. This simple story is how I got the name for this cookbook.

Circling The Rabbit

So you and your mate got up early this morning, cooked some brekkie, cleaned up the campsite, got the bait and the rods out and headed off to do a spot of fishin' for the day. I bet you got a shock when you returned to camp later in the day only to find someone else had been there and took everything including your tuckerbox. I reckon you'd be pretty mad. I know I would. Never mind, I know you're hungry and tired, but there is a way of getting a good evening meal with no gear at all. If this happens to you, well try this idea, it works.

How to do it

First of all you have to find a rabbit, and hopefully it will be sitting in a cleared spot. Now you have to walk in a big circle. Start out at about 30–40 feet from the rabbit, walking constantly and getting closer to the rabbit all the time.

Now you can't rush it—just take your time, remembering this might be your last chance for a good meal for quite a while. If you have a friend circling with you at an equal distance apart, it is much easier to get the rabbit mesmerised.

Now up until this point, things are going pretty well. The rabbit is sitting, but you're getting tired and anxious, and the next bit is the hard bit. As you get within grabbing distance of the rabbit you shouldn't make any sudden moves, except for the one and only chance you will get to grab the rabbit for your next meal. When you reckon you're ready to take your chance, grab him. If you've caught him, you done real good.

See it was easy.

How To Humanely Kill A Rabbit

So you caught him alive, hope he didn't scratch you. Now, to dispatch him easily and painlessly, follow Yattie's way to humanely kill your rabbit.

How to do it

Grab the rabbit by the rear legs in one hand, lifting him clear off the ground, with your other hand cupped and firmly closed over the top of the rabbit's head, laying an ear down each side of the rabbit's shoulder.

Kink the rabbit's head back, attempting to reach 90% down to its backbone, and stretching the rabbit firmly overall at the same time. While under pressure, screw the rabbit's head to the side. This dislocates the neck, severing its vitals, inflicting immediate and painless death.

Gutting And Skinning A Rabbit

Now that you have killed your rabbit, you need to gut it within 15 minutes—you see, the body gases could build up and spoil the meat. This is Yattie's way of gutting and skinning a rabbit. If you don't have a knife or anything sharp with you, why not use the rabbit's own sharp claw—well, it's not a bad idea.

Ingredients

One rabbit
One sharp knife

How to gut it

Hold the rabbit's front section belly up between you knees. Grab the belly fur 1 1/2 inches from its vent. Make a cut crossways 1 inch from the vent, just under the skin, 2 inches long, exposing the belly flesh. Pull the skin upwards, which should separate the skin from the belly flesh. Make a 2-inch cut longways opening the belly cavity. Just follow the line visible on the flesh. Use only the tip of a sharp knife to avoid puncturing the intestines. Should this occur, wash spillage immediately after gutting. Through this cut the insides may be removed by hand.

Another method of gutting after opening is to grasp the rabbit by the head in one hand, and just below the ribs with the other, drawing down in a stripping movement until all insides are removed. Once perfected, this is a tidy method.

How to skin it

Hold the rabbit belly-up between your knees. Extend a 2-inch cut up inside of each rear leg to the base of the paw, cutting the skin only. The thumbs are used to part the skin from the hind legs. When legs are skinned, exposing the buttocks at the base of the tail and backbone down to the paws, trim skin at paws running knife under skin as far as possible towards rabbit's claws. Cut the tail bone off at the base of the spine.

Grasping the rabbit by the skin at the exposed end, release the knee hold, place the rabbit's rear paws under your foot and pull up. The skin will run upwards from its body to its front legs, exposing them. Cut the skin at the front legs and pull it over its neck. Cut off the head with the whole skin attached.

If the skin is not being used, remove the paws with a sharp knife at the knee joints. Cut the anal tunnel between the hind legs, removing unwanted organs and dark coloured game glands each side of the tail bone (failure to remove these glands may render meat strong and unpalatable).

The rabbit's flavour can be improved if it is hung (skinned or unskinned) in a shady position away from flies, or overnight, depending on temperature.

He's now ready for the pot.

ONIONS BEAT ALL

Your good pocket knife gone rusty? Well stick the blade into an onion for about half an hour, then give it a good wash. Hopefully the rust will come off.

A Rabbit On A Shovel

Now that you have caught your rabbit and you're highly excited about your performance because you reckoned that circling bit wouldn't work and it did, and you're that hungry you could eat him raw, well don't. Here is the original Rabbit On A Shovel Recipe.

Ingredients

One rabbit
A few good spoonfuls of margarine
A couple of spoonfuls of salt
1/4 pannikin of vinegar
1/2 bucket of water

How to do it

After skinning, gutting and rinsing your rabbit, and making sure the tail is removed, cut it into quarters. Mix the salt and vinegar in the water, and add the rabbit quarters and soak for a couple of hours.

Have your fire burn down to coals. Take your shovel to a good size stump and give the shovel a couple of good old belts, to get rid of any dirt or whatever. If you're real fussy, give the shovel a scrub.

Next, heat the shovel by placing it over the hot coals. Melt some margarine on it, put in the rabbit quarters, turning every now and then to ensure even cooking. He's cooked when a fork easily pierces the flesh.

While eating and enjoying your *RABBIT ON A SHOVEL*, cast your mind back to the early Australian pioneers. This is how they used to do it.

French Rabbit *A La Fair Dinkum*

The French love it, they reckon it's tops in England, it's now up to the Aussies to give it a go.

Ingredients

1 rabbit
2 or 3 rashers of bacon
6 small onions
Good spoonful of flour
A couple of shakes of garlic
Salt and pepper
Water

How to do it

Skin, gut, clean and cut rabbit into pieces and soak him overnight in salt water.

Get your pan hot while dicing bacon and onions. Brown bacon in pan and remove. Put rabbit pieces into pan and lightly fry (do not brown). Remove rabbit. Add flour, mix well, add 1/2 pint of hot water and cook the sauce for a few minutes.

Turn into camp oven with browned bacon, rabbit, onions and garlic. Add a pannikin of hot water and bring to the boil. Put the lid on and let it simmer away for about 1 1/2 hours.

Put onto your plate with some fair-dinkum *AUSSIE DAMPER*.

Jugged Hare

This is a ripper old way of cooking up a young hare if you ever happen to get one, and they are not real bad either. A hare is about twice the size of a rabbit, and longer and stronger.

Ingredients

1 young hare
A couple of onions
A big pinch of pepper
A splash of lemon concentrate
Some margarine
Some flour
2 good slurps of tomato sauce
Hot water
A small slurp of Tabasco sauce
Some wine, if any

How to do it

Skin, gut and rinse well your young hare then cut him into small bits, flouring each piece.

Put into a hot camp oven with diced onions, pepper and a splash of lemon and cover with hot water. Let simmer until tender (check with a fork).

Take hare out of the camp oven and thicken the gravy with margarine and flour, add sauces and wine and let boil for another 10 minutes.

Pour the gravy over the bits on your plate. This is how they used to do it the old country.

Roasted Underground Mutton

The old rabbit is good tucker at the best of times, but when he's stuffed and roasted he's just a bit better than beaut.

Ingredients

1 rabbit
1/2 pannikin of breadcrumbs
1 small onion diced
1 small apple peeled and grated
Salt and pepper
A good spoonful of margarine

How to do it

Skin, gut and clean the rabbit. Mix all the other bits together and put 'em inside the rabbit, and bring opening together with meat skewers to hold stuffing in place.

Put the rabbit in a well-greased camp oven and cook, turning occasionally. When a fork pierces his flesh easily he's ready.

Serve with *Spud Pie* for a bush meal with class.

Rabbit From The South

I tell you what, the old rabbit cooked this way sure tastes different. It takes a bit of time to prepare but the end result is well worth the wait.

Ingredients

1 rabbit (for best results 3/4 grown)
Plain flour
1 egg
Breadcrumbs
Big splash of cooking oil
Water

How to do it

Take the rabbit, if you got one. Skin, gut, clean and cut into pieces. Put him into the camp oven with water and boil gently for 1 1/2 hours. Leave rabbit in the water to cool—this keeps it moist.

Remove when cool. Cover pieces with plain flour. Put your pan over the fire to heat. Coat rabbit pieces with egg then roll in breadcrumbs. Fry in hot oil until golden brown.

Serve him with some mashed spuds.

Rabbit Has Been Flattened

I don't know about you, but I like a feed of rabbit every now and then, and this is another way of cooking him up, and it doesn't take much time either. And no, he didn't get run over by a truck.

Ingredients

1 rabbit
Some flour
A good pinch of salt
A small pinch of pepper
1 egg
2 slices of bread beaten to crumbs
1 good-sized onion
1/2 pannikin of cooking oil

How to do it

After you have caught your rabbit, skin, gut and clean him and cut into very small bits. Mix breadcrumbs with a very finely-chopped onion, salt and pepper. Cover rabbit bits well, an ice-cream container is ideal for this. Roll into balls the size of golf balls, and flatten in flour. Cook in hot oil in the frypan, occasionally turning.

When it's ready, put heaps of *Scrub Relish* on it, and have it with some spuds as well.

Cottontail

When you come home to the camp
And you're worn out with the cramp
And the missus won't cook
And you're feelin' a bit crook
There's only one thing to do
And that's go for the stew
It's a rabbit of course
And it's better than horse.

Ingredients

A rabbit
A few strips of bacon
Half pannikin of flour
2 pannikins of stock (beef or chicken)
Few shakes of mixed herbs
Salt and pepper
Tablespoon of margarine

How to do it

Skin, gut and rinse clean the rabbit, don't forget to cut the tail bit out. Dice the bacon, have your bush barbie or pan hot and fry the rabbit in a little margarine, when done transfer both to a hot Bedourie oven or a big saucepan, add the stock, salt and pepper and mixed herbs, let him cook (simmer) until he's tender. Remove from the oven add some flour to thicken, if you have some wine pour in a few good splashes. Give the gravy one more boil; keep a close eye on it, if the gravy is to thick add some water

Serve the good old cottontail with some spuds and pour gravy over the lot.

GRILLING — IT'S ALL IN THE FLAMES

When grilling your tucker, the best tip of all is to have a good fire at first and then let it burn down as your cooking progresses. If you have a flamy fire, throw a handful of salt in, this will reduce the flames and you are ready to grill. If you have a dull fire, it hardens the meat which makes it horrible. A smoking fire gives a smoky flavour—don't think much of smoked rabbit.

Shoehorn (did this ever happen?)

Years ago two mates were standing around having a yarn. One bloke says, "My brother, the pup and I got 4 pair of bunnies the other day." By the time the other bloke got to the pub the rumour was, his mate Ralph had netted 30 pair and had seen something strange. That's how quickly tall stories travel around the bush.

Meanwhile there was another rumour circulating through the same small town of a giant rabbit that was terrorising the area. The story says big Flopsy was too big and strong for the dogs and that he was too clever for even the smartest of rabbiters.

I heard about this story just recently and started asking questions about whether the story was fair dinkum or not. My small investigation led me to meet a bloke named Johnno, an old ex-barman. Johnno and his wife invited me to their place for a barbecue and he promised to tell me the story as he knew it. After we had finished our barbie, Old Johnno sat down on a chair, took off his hat and started to tell his tale.

"Mate your going to find this hard to believe, I reckon it's for real, plus I have some proof," he said.

"It all happened about 50 years ago. One afternoon I was working behind the bar when this rough-looking, bearded old bloke covered in blood came in for a beer. He was rotten as a chop, he stank like a dead polecat, his eyes were a steely grey colour, his hands were constantly shaking and I noticed a small letter branded just above his wrist.

" 'What do you do for a quid?' I asked. The old bloke said, 'I'm a rabbologist and I'm cleaning out a joint just up the road.' 'Hey boys, this bloke's a rabbologist!' I yelled. The bar roared with laughter.

"A few minutes later the old bloke said, 'Seen something today that scared the crap out of me.' I thought, this bloke's had a few, but it's worth a listen. 'What did you see?' I asked. The old bloke took his time, rolled a fag, shuffled around on his stool, and then said, 'I saw the biggest, half starved, in-bred mongrel of a so-called rabbit I've ever seen, bigger than an Alsatian dog, when he hopped his stride was longer than a Kangaroo's, his thigh muscles were bigger than a pro. boxer's, he had ears longer than a mule's, his tail would bend any car aerial, when he turned his back he had a pair bigger than a rogue Shetland pony's, but most of all, his buck teeth, they were that big you could use them as a shoehorn.' 'What? Is this fair dinkum?' "" I asked.

"The boys in the bar, they were beside themselves, they were all rolling around on the floor in uncontrollable laughter.

"I gave the old bloke a fresh beer and said, 'Tell us what happened.' By this time we had about 30 blokes in a circle just itching to hear the next lot of verbal garbage the old bloke was trying to flog us.

"The rabbologist took a swig out of his fresh beer and said, 'When I first spotted him I couldn't believe it, he was about 50 feet away and he was staring me out, then he started moving towards me, he rolled his bottom lip like a camel, grunted at me like a sick goose, stamped his back leg, then charged, but I was too smart for him, I jumped into the ute and said to myself "Gotta get off the bottle, rabbits are not bred to attack like dogs".

'For the next few minutes he was stalking me like a tom cat lining up a mouse. The very next moment, and in a huge cloud of dust a ute arrived, it was the cocky and his dog. I said, "Look at the size of big Flopsy." The cocky said, "I've heard stories about this bloke, he's been giving the dogs hell for a few weeks now." The old cocky, he's smart, he didn't get out of his ute either. His dog, which was a cross between a Russian staghound, bluc heeler and Doberman, was going ape droppings in the back, trying to rip the chain out of the ute.

'The cocky quietly got out of the ute, unclipped the chain and yelled to the dog, "Go get boy, he's only a rabbit." The dog, frothing at the mouth and barking his brains out launched himself over the side of ute and charged towards the rabbit. The rabbit seen him coming and charged head-on toward the dog. "Boy, this is going to be good," I said to the cocky. When the two protagonists got close to one another they both jumped high into the air clashed in a bone jamming head on collision, a perfect introduction, they reminded me of a pair of unco-ordinated ballet dancers.

'They crashed to the ground both dazed. After a few seconds they got up, had a shake, then all hell broke loose, the dirt's flying, the blood's flowing, the rabbit's grunting like a pig, the dog's bellowing like a bull calf, they're locked together in a show of strength, the cocky's running around in circles with a shotgun screaming his head off at the dog, I'm jumping up and down and barracking like hell for the winner. "This is better than the fights at the West Melbourne Stadium,", I said. A mob of Galahs in the paddock next door, the noise is to much for them and they take off, a couple of old Merino rams watching on reckon they could be next. They charge through a fence with fright and head off down the highway. I reckon I'm going to have a heart attack so I jump into the ute and head for the hills to pack up my skins. After a while I returned to the fight scene to find out what happened.'

"The old bloke then went quiet. 'Well, what happened?' I snapped. The bar was in silence. You could hear a pin drop. The old bloke eased his rickety old frame off the stool and said, 'I'm going to the dunny.' A few minutes passed and I went to the dunny to check on him and, when I came back, one of the boys said, 'Where is he?' 'He's gone,' I said. Then the nasty remarks – 'What a load of crap', 'Been on the grog too long' and all that type of stuff.

"The next thing, a hell of a commotion outside the door of the ladies' lounge, I raced out to see what's going on, no-one there, only a small cardboard box on the doorstop. I picked up the box and went back inside. One of the derro drinkers blurted out, 'What's in the box?' I opened it up and looked inside and couldn't believe my eyes. I pulled out a pearl-white object with a slight bend; it was 6 or 7 inches long, about an inch wide, it had a green tinge on the rough end and was a reddish colour on the smooth end. Actually it looked very much like an expensive ladies ivory shoehorn. Also in the box was a broken buckle, it looked like part of a huge dog's collar.

"Silence once again overtook the pub, all the blokes had a look at the objects, not many comments were made and within minutes the bar was empty." Johnno lowered his head, lent back into his chair and closed his eyes.

"Is this fair dinkum Johnno," I asked. "What a story; a bit hard to swallow, but why don't you take it to a TV station?"

Johnno's wife disappeared into the house, a few minutes later she emerged wearing one of those animal skin capes that ladies used to wear. "Beautiful skin, what is it?" I asked, Johnno pipes up, "Have a good look mate, it's a rabbit skin, not a join, a *lone* skin." "Look at its size, bigger than a huge dog, where did you get it?" I asked. "My wife got it from and old cocky long before I met her; *his* brother had given the cape to him," Johnno said. "The cocky told her the cape had 8 skins all sewn together. Here, you check it." I examined it closely and I couldn't see a seam or a join, it appeared to be one huge skin. However, feeling through the lining, I could feel some form of a protrusion. I did see a small letter which looked like an {R} branded near the top of the skin. "Johnno, could this be invisible sewing?" I asked. "No. Checked that," he replied. I had to ask the questions: "Do you reckon this skin came from the giant rabbit? What's the cocky's name? What happened to the rabbologist, did he ever exist? Did the dog survive? Who was the cocky that gave your wife the cape? What happened to the shoehorn and the broken buckle and what happened to Flopsy?" Johnno just shrugged his shoulders and said, "I don't know any more, and it has never been mentioned since that afternoon."

We have all heard stories about feral cats and mice, the other day I heard a bloke on the wireless mouthing off about feral chooks. Can anybody help me solve this mystery? I would love to see the elusive shoehorn and dog' collar. Is this story for real or is it just a yarn only old blokes can spin?

Yabbies & Crays

Chuck 'em back

When you're out fishin' and yabby'n and havin' a great time
Keepin' little fish or a yabby with eggs—that's a crime
Chuck 'em right back and be fair and be pure
They will all grow next year and be good game for sure.

Crays in shells

Do you remember what it's like, sitting under a big old gum tree, a couple of fishing lines in the water, listening to the love calls of some screeching corellas overhead, having a doze and sipping a nice cold one and waiting for a good-sized fish to come by. You get a slight touch on the rod, spring to attention, spill your drink, bump your head and say to your mate "Someone is knocking on my door", wait a moment, haul in the line, WHAT! Have a go at the tangle, in the middle of the mess is a purler of a Murray cray, cut him out, put him into the Esky, then your devious mind swings into gear, rebait the line and try and catch a few more, which you do. Your brain is now in overdrive, you have a plan, clean yourself up and head for camp and say to your girlfriend "Luv, got something special for tea tonight. You'll love it.' 'Oh Yeah,' she says, then whispers and laughs to your mate's girlfriend.

Ingredients

Murray crays (make sure theyre legal)

1 pannikin of milk

Some salt

Spoonful or 2 of flour

Curry powder

How to do it

After dipping the crays into the boiling water remove and let cool, take all the meat out and put to one side, keep the shells, thoroughly wash, clean and dry, put on to a plate for presentation (do you like that). Heat the pan, pour in milk and bring to the boil, add flour and curry powder, cook until it thickens taste for seasoning, add salt if required, add Cray meat bit by bit to the mixture, cook until done.

Serving now this critical, spoon the Cray meat into the nice clean shells, pour some of mixture over, and decorate the plate with tomato slices. Present the plate with a fork with your lady friend on a folded-up tea towel together with a glass of wine, and then whisper something sweet in her ear. She'll love it. (maybe).

Yabbies

When I was a little kid, my mate and I spent most of our summers walking or riding horses from dam to dam with our little cotton lines and bits of meat on the end for bait. We always said "Mum we're going to get you some yabbies". Most times we did, that is, if we didn't get sidetracked and, as you know, this often happens with kids.

Everybody knows how to cook yabbies, chuck them into a bucket of boiling water and cook until they turn red, shell, salt and pepper and pig out. Some people dip them in mayonnaise or seafood dressing.

Here is a different way of cooking them.

Ingredients

Yabbies

Some strips of bacon

Some shredded cheese

Cooking oil

Worcestershire sauce

Pickled onions (if available)

How to do it

After cooking the yabbies, strip out the meat and devain, partly cook the bacon, wrap the yabby meat in a piece of bacon, thread on to a skewer, add a pickled onion if you have some, keep adding pieces until skewer is full, brush with Worcestershire sauce. Place on an oiled hot plate and grill, turning regularly. When nearly done, sprinkle shredded cheese over to melt.

Serve straight away.

Fish — Cooking Up Your Catch

To Skin And Fillet A Fish

To a lot of people, skinning and filleting a fish can be a major task. Here are some simple and easy ideas to help you make that task so much easier.

To skin a fish

First of all you need a fish. Not an easy task sometimes, but keep trying, one will come along directly.

When one does come along, you can begin skinning by cutting around the head, then down its back and across the tail then up the front on both sides.

Free the skin at the head and pull down to the tail on both sides.

It was easy eh, not a problem?

To fillet a fish

The experts say the easiest way is to place one hand on the fish and insert a flat sharp knife in the opening near the head and slice the knife along the backbone towards the tail. This takes the flesh off in one piece. Repeat the procedure on the other side. Remove all small bones.

He's now ready for the pan.

FISH SCALING MADE EASIER

After gutting, dip the fish into boiling water for a few seconds before removing scales. This will help the scales come off easier.

A Fish In A Hubcap

Fish in a hubcap you say! I tell you what, it's happened before, and I reckon if you've lost your frypan the next best thing to use is a good old-fashioned hubcap. After all, if you have some freshly-caught fish and you want the fish for brekkie, you'll use anything. And why not? Make sure the hubcap is steel and not plastic or it may melt.

Ingredients

One large fish
1 egg
1 pinch of salt
Breadcrumbs
1/2 pannikin of flour
Small pinch of pepper
Big splash of cooking oil

How to do it

Take your fish—if you have caught one—scale, gut and fillet. Dip your fillets into flour seasoned with salt and pepper, then into the beaten egg or milk, then into breadcrumbs.

Now if you've lost your frypan, rip the steel hubcap off the family chariot and give it a real good scrub-out.

Pour the cooking oil into your hot hubcap frypan, then pop in the fish pieces and fry, turning occasionally. Cook until golden brown, or until the flesh lifts easily with a fork.

Serve with chips cooked in the hubcap as well.

DJ's Baked Fish

My Dear wife of over 36 years is a living legend when it comes to baking and stuffing a fish. I've tried for years to find out exactly what spices and additives she uses, she just says "ask my grandmother, it's her recipe and it came from Scotland". "Yeah, good one". Anyway, below is an idea of what she uses; this one is pretty good but not as good as hers.

Ingredients

A good sized mullet or cod.
1 spoonful of margarine 1 egg
2 anchovies fillets (if any)
Some Lemon juice
Some salt
1 pannikin of bread crumbs
2 pinches of mixed herbs
1 small diced onion
1 pinch cayenne pepper
Aluminium foil

How to do it

To make the stuffing mix, margarine, mixed herbs, diced onions, 3 pinches of salt, 1 pinch of cayenne pepper, bread crumbs, beaten egg and chopped up anchovies are combined until a smooth mixture is obtained.

Take the fish, scale, and gut, clean and wash well; dry thoroughly and leave the head on. Stuff the fish and sew up with butcher's string or fine wire. Rub lemon juice and salt over the fish, roll fish in aluminium foil ensuring complete closure. Dig a hole under the fire and lay plenty of hot coals in the hole, lay fish in hole and pull the fire back. Cooking should take an hour or two but keep your eye on it. When done serve with roasted spuds in foil, for a top feed

Another couple of ways of doing this delicious meal is in the camp oven or at home in the kitchen oven. It's fantastic.

Camp Oven Cod

By crikey I bet you worked hard to catch this bloke, especially after all the time and effort you put into him. Now do yourself and your mates a favour and take the time and effort to cook him properly. I suggest you cook him this way.

Ingredients

1 kilo of fresh cod
1 onion
1 packet of soup mix
1 bare pannikin milk
Some grated cheese
A dob of margarine
A big spoon of flour

How to do it

First of all gut, scale and fillet the fish. Then boil until cooked.

Put the pan on and cut up the onion and fry it in some margarine and thicken with a big spoonful of flour and milk. Shred the boiled fish into the hot camp oven with the fried onion and thickening and add the packet of soup mix. Stir until it thickens. Top with grated cheese and let cook until the cheese melts.

When ready serve with mashed potato or *EDWARD RIVER SCONES*.

TASTIER FISH FRIES

When frying fish, chuck a little bit of curry powder into your frypan, it improves the flavour and also improves the colour.

Drunken Carp (Queen of the river)

Carp, we hate them in Australia, when we catch one it goes straight up the bank and get it's head cut off. In Europe, carp are one of the more sought after inland fish. Fisherman actually pay hard earned cash to try and catch them. To cook them in Australia they have a lousy record. In Europe they bake them, stew them, fry them and even put them on the menu in some restaurants.

Ingredients

1 carp
3 cans of beer
Lemon juice
Some margarine or dripping
Handful of salt
Pepper
Flour
Bucked of water

How to do it

When you catch this slimy, unwanted mongrel of a thing, chuck it up the bank and chop its head off then hang it to bleed, scale and gut it, then chuck it into a bucket of salty water. In Europe they say "to thoroughly cleanse" you only need one can of beer to cook the fish and 2 cans to prepare yourself to eat it, open one now. Take the knife to "the queen of the river" that's what they call them in Europe, cut a few slabs of flesh of each side, rub the slabs into some seasoned flour and add a few drops of lemon juice. At this particular stage of proceedings in Europe we would be 'inserting some delicate forcemeat into the carp'.

Melt some margarine into the pan, add the fish pieces, pour in a can of beer and put the lid on and let it cook for a while, turn and let simmer until the flesh lifts easily with a fork. Have the last can.

If you're cooking for some of your mates don't tell them what it is, they'll probably say 'Bloody good tucker mate'.

In Europe they say 'Garnish the dish with parsley and the sauce in a boat'

How the hell would I know, I'm only repeating what the experts have said.

Redyellowbonywhite

Four blokes were sitting outside a local general store. One bloke says, the reddies are going off the planet on worms, I got 35 in 2 hours yesterday. The second bloke who is a bit of a blowhard says, that's nothing, the yellows are jumping into the boat up north, I got 40 in an I hour and a half. Sitting beside our Aussie heroes is a Stetson-hatted rooster from overseas. He says. 'Laast week I was fishing in the territory, the barramundi were going that good I just gave them a whistle and they came a swimming, only had to pick them up, I got 45 in 1 hour. The fourth bloke, a quiet and shy fellow from northern part of the old country said, when I was in Van Diemens land recently I beached a big one with a giant fin on his back, when I opened him up I got a couple of 10 pound snappers, 16 salmon, 50 cans of sardines and a right foot work boot, I'm now looking for a left foot size 7 work boot to match, as well as a bottle of sauce for the sardines.

Do you believe this?

If you do and somehow manage to land a decent size fish, go to the general store and stretch this story a bit further. In the meantime you still have to cook up your catch; try this way

Ingredients

A couple of fillets of fish	**1 bottle of cooking oil**
Half a pannikin of flour	**Some beer**
Some soda water	**1 egg**
A couple of spuds	**Salt and Pepper**

How to do it

To make the batter. In a bowl, tip in some flour; add a beaten egg and salt and pepper, splash in some beer and soda water, mix well until smooth and slightly runny, let stand. Pour oil into a large saucepan and get it really hot. Peel, wash and dry the spuds and cut into small slices, put into hot oil, dip fillets into batter, coat well and drain, place fillets into oil, then fry until golden brown and the chips are crisp.
Serve with Salt and Pepper and Lemon Juice.

Bull Kelp Salmon

About 50 years ago the old bloke and myself were down Warrnambool way looking to buy a horse, naturally we went fishing to get something to eat and with luck we landed a nice sized salmon about 3 pound. The old feller said, "Boy go and get some of that bull kelp and wash it really well in the sea and bring it up here, donít drop it in the sand". "No, Dad," I said and, as kids did in those days, I done what I was told. I'm thinking to myself, "I hope were not having fried bull kelp for tea."

Ingredients

1 good sized salmon
Some dripping
Some Salt
Plenty of clean bull kelp

How he done it

He first bled, scaled, gutted and washed the salmon in sea water. Then he generously rubbed him inside and out with dripping. He wrapped him tightly in the wet bull kelp insuring that he was completely covered. Of course we had a purler of a fire going, he dug a hole under the fire and put a lot of red hot coals into the bottom of the hole. He then laid the kelp covered fish on top of the coals, covered the fish with more kelp, pulled back the fire and let him steam for a couple of hours. He then checked, freshened the fire and waited until he was done. When ready we tipped some salt on him and tucked in. He tasted a lot better than fried seaweed.

When we got home I said to mum, "Can you teach me how to cook and put together a small tucker box of food for me? I'm getting sick of eating that half-cooked stuff that the old feller is bashing up."

Steamed Fish In White Sauce

If you've had a real tough night and you are feeling a bit ordinary, here is an excellent meal that may help you to recover just that bit quicker. But no guarantees.

Ingredients

1 fish
1 big dob of margarine
1 pinch of salt
A touch of lemon concentrate
2 large spoonfuls of water
White Sauce

How to do it

Scale, gut and fillet your fish and put into a bucket of salty water for 1/4 hour.

Dry fish and put into a greased moderately-hot camp oven. Sprinkle with salt and lemon, add margarine, and leave for about 10 minutes. Test by running a skewer or knife through thickest part, which should be soft.

Cover with *White Sauce* and a touch of lemon juice and serve with mashed spuds.

Tassie Pearl

My mate Ted lives in Tassie and is an oyster maniac like me. The last time I was at Ted's place he said to me, 'lets go and get some oysters for tea', 'good idea' It took us about half and hour to find his private spot. 'Where are the oysters?' 'You're standing on them you idiot'. Fair dinkum they were massive in size and there were acres of them. 'Come over here mate and look at these, just our size'. We got a couple of buckets of them and headed back to his place to cook them up. Here is Ted's way of cooking oysters, but I love them natural with a home made sauce.

Ted's Oysters in the pan

Ingredients

Oysters
Cayenne Pepper
Lemon Juice
Some Salt
2 eggs
Margarine
1 pannikin of bread crumbs
Some flour

How he done it

Beat the eggs and put on a plate, put bread crumbs on another plate, add some flour to another plate, remove oysters from shells, sprinkle with lemon juice and cayenne pepper, dip oysters into flour, then the egg and bread crumbs, heat the pan and melt in some margarine, add oysters, turn now and then until cooked. Serve with salt and lemon juice. We had about a dozen each and not one of them worked.

Oysters natural with home-made sauce

Ingredients and how to do it

Spoonful of Worcestershire sauce, 2 spoonfuls of tomato sauce, 2,3 or 4 drops of Tabasco sauce some pepper and some cream. Mix the lot together until a nice and creamy mixture is formed, remove oysters from their shells and dip into mixture. Boy they're good.

Sweeney's Fish In The Mud

This is a different way of cooking up that catch as a succulent meal. In the Northern Territory this is the way they do it. Use yellowbelly, barramundi, cod or any other you catch.

Ingredients

1 whole fish
A supply of mud or clay

How to do it

First of all catch the fish, dispatch it, then completely cover it with a 1-inch layer of mud or clay. Dig a hole under the coals of the campfire, place the mud-coated fish in the hole and completely pull back the fire. Leave for a while.

Dig the fish from under the coals and let it cool. The mud casing will be hard and cracked. Carefully remove the casing—the skin and scales will peel away with the mud, leaving the lovely fish which has been cooked in its own juices. The gut will be a small lump inside; throw it away.

Serve with lemon juice.

Waterhole Fish

Here is another way of cooking fish, it takes a bit of effort, but any good meal is worth the extra effort, especially if you have just landed a goodie.

Ingredients

Fish fillets from a 2-pounder
1 medium chopped onion
Some garlic granules
3 good-sized chopped tomatoes
1/2 pannikin of plain flour
Salt and pepper
Good splash of cooking oil

How to do it

Put your pan on to heat. Mix flour with some salt and pepper. Cut the fish fillets into small squares and cover them in the flour. Pop some cooking oil into your hot pan and fry the fish pieces until brown on both sides.

When done, put the fish pieces onto a plate and keep hot. Fry the onion until nearly cooked then add tomatoes and a couple of shakes of garlic granules and cook for 4–5 minutes.

When done pour contents of pan over fish and serve with scones or damper.

Birds — Wild & Tame

Hunters and Shooters Beware

There's one thing in this world that's a worry to me
That's a man with a gun that reckons he can be
A hero to his mates and he's probably havin' a ball
Who blasts away at anything—anything at all
Our great Australian bush is the best there is around
Just one stray bullet can knock nature to the ground
It really needs protecting and it isn't really a game
Put your gun in its case mate or be careful where you aim.

Roast Camp Oven Chook

Everybody has their own ideas about cooking the traditional Sunday Roast. This is an old shearer's cook's way of doing it in the camp oven.

Ingredients

1 good sized chook

A few pinches salt and pepper

A few drops of Lemon Juice

3 or 4 slices of bread

1 good sized onion

2 good spoonfuls of margarine

A few shakes of mixed herbs

Small amount of flour

Some milk

How to do it

To make the stuffing, chop the bread to make some crumbs, stir in the mixed herbs, salt and pepper, rub in a spoonful of margarine, moisten with a few drops of lemon juice and a small amount of milk until the stuffing becomes workable.

The chook

Wash and wipe the chook and salt inside, stuff the chook. Have your camp oven hot, rub margarine salt and pepper over the chook then slice and place onion rings on top for more flavour. Place camp oven into the coals and put some hot coals on the lid, cook until ready.

You can roast your spuds, pumpkin or what ever vegies you have with your chook or cook them in the coals.

When the chook is done to your liking, remove the fat, add some flour and a small amount of water to the juices in the camp oven, stir and bring to the boil, simmer for a couple of minutes for a tasty gravy, serve hot.

Wild Fowl Stew

If you can get hold of some chicken pieces or a whole chook, and it's Sunday, well don't hang around, cook it up and get into it. I bet you eggs-to-young'ns you'll love it.

Ingredients

4 kilos chicken pieces
2 good spoonfuls of margarine
5 rashers of bacon, chopped
12 small onions
A good shake of garlic granules
190 g tin of mushrooms
1/2 pannikin of plain flour
2 chicken stock cubes
3 pannikins of water
Salt and pepper
2 pannikins of red wine if available

How to do it

Put half of your margarine into a hot camp oven, add peeled whole onions and chopped bacon and cook until onions are light brown. Add chicken pieces to camp oven and brown on all sides. Add mushrooms, garlic, remaining margarine, salt and pepper. Sprinkle in flour, stir well. Slowly add water, red wine and stock cubes. Stir until thickened.

Cover and bake until chicken is tender.

When ready serve with *Aussie Damper* or *Bushies' Fried Scones.*

Stuffed duck 'A LA ORANGE'

Try this out, but not the way my mate Bazza and I did one Sunday. The phone rang: "Bazza here, got a couple of ducks, get the fire going, see ya". He arrived and we got started, done everything right except the cans kept coming, we put the ducks on at 4, took them out at 8, when we lifted the lid off the camp oven. To our surprise, we only had 2 little burnt objects, no sign of a duck. So we had a vegemite sanga for tea. But good fun.

Ingredients

A Couple of ducks
Some dripping
An orange
Some water
Some Salt & Pepper
A couple of onions
2 spoonfuls of flour
Some garlic

How to do it

After you have plucked, cleaned, washed and dried your ducks thoroughly, mix the dripping, garlic, salt and pepper. Rub the mixture over the ducks inside and out, peel the orange and onion cut into quarters and put into the ducks. Put the ducks into the camp oven and place into your cooking fire, put some coals onto the lid and let cook for an hour or so. (For timing ask my mate Bazza)

When done remove ducks from the oven and keep warm while you make the gravy. Remove all the fat, put some flour and water into the juices left in the bottom, stir until it boils, then simmer until a nice consistency is formed, add more water if required.

When done serve with Ernie's vegies.

Bidsey's Crumbed Wild Duck

This is my mother's favourite way to cook a duck. She got the recipe from her mum, so it goes back a few years now, and has filled many a man's empty belly.

Ingredients

A couple of ducks
Some salt and pepper
Some plain flour
A couple of beaten eggs
Breadcrumbs
Big splash of cooking oil

How to do it

Take the ducks and pluck, clean, wash and then thoroughly dry. With a knife, divide into portions. Roll the portions in the flour seasoned with salt and pepper, completely covering.

Dip the portions in the beaten eggs then roll in the breadcrumbs. If desired, a sprinkle of mixed herbs in the breadcrumbs adds extra flavour—if you reckon it's worth it, it sure helps.

Have your frypan hot and add the cooking oil. Cook the duck portions slowly until tender.

Serve with peas and *Spud Pie*.

Bazza's Pan Fried Quackers

My mate Bazza is a fair dinkum, laid back old fashioned Aussie type of a bloke and he's pretty handy when it comes time to knocking up a feed. After our episode with the roasted ducks he had a go at these the next day.

Ingredients

Couple of ducks
1 onion
Few good shakes of garlic granules
Few drops of Tabasco sauce
Half a can of beer
Cooking oil
Spoonful of margarine
Salt & pepper
2 rashers of bacon

How to do it (Bazza's way)

"Hey Lummo lets cook these quackers." "OK, what do you want me to do?" "Clean' em, wash' em, dry' em, hack' em into bits, press' em flat , here use a shovel, cut the bacon and onion into bits". "Done that; now what?" "Mix this up and rub' em all over." "What is it?". "Margarine, garlic, salt, pepper and more garlic (Bazza likes garlic). Lummo where's the wine? haven't got any." So he is off to the esky. "The pan's hot, got the oil in and we'll put some beer in instead of the wine. Here's the onion and bacon, in they go." A couple of minutes go by, Bazza's sitting on a stump drinking a can, then jumps up, "Stone the crows, the quackers!", so he chucks the quackers in and starts pouring the liquid over for a few minutes, then turns them and does the same again, he then puts in a few drops of Tabasco sauce and stirs the whole lot up and says "That'll fire em up. Quackers are done, you serve em, I'm stuffed." "OK mate." He also cooked up a tin of asparagus and boiled some spuds. It was fantastic. Do yourself a favour and give this one a try.

Flappy Green

This is different and it's dead set easy. When you're sick of stews and roasts and have a few wild ducks left, try this, it doesn't look much but you can live on it.

Ingredients

Couple of cold pre-cooked ducks

1 pkt dried peas

Salt and pepper

Couple of pannikins of gravy

Couple drops of lemon juice

How to do it

Gravy mix

Mix up a gravox mix, your own special or the same one as in "Bazza's pan fried duck". To fire it up add a few slurps of Worcestershire sauce, either way will do the trick.

The ducks

In your billy or saucepan, half fill it with water and bring it to the boil and add a couple of good pinches of salt and empty a pkt of dried peas and let it simmer for a few minutes or so, until the peas are par cooked, don't overcook the peas.

Have your frypan hot, put in the gravy mix with a small amount of margarine, gently divide the pre-cooked ducks into small pieces, put in the ducks, together with the par-cooked peas, season with salt and pepper and simmer for a short time, then add a few drops of lemon juice.

Serve the duck pieces on toast, pour the gravy and peas over the top and wash down with billy tea.

Pigeon Pieces in Gravy

This is the old fashioned way of cooking pigeons. 100 years ago, pigeons and other small birds were a delicacy for the rich and famous, but over the years, times and tastes have changed.

Ingredients

Margarine **Water** **Salt and pepper**

Couple of rashers of bacon **1 chopped onion** **Some flour**

How they used to do it

Pluck, gut and clean the birds and cut into pieces and remove bones. Heat the fry pan and put in some margarine and get it hot, real hot. Lay the bird pieces in the pan inside out and cook for a few minutes then turn, when cooked remove birds and add the onion and bacon to the pan and cook, add salt and pepper. Put in some flour and start stirring, add some water and keep stirring. Return the bird pieces to the pan and cook until the gravy is formed, if to thick add more water.

Serve with damper for a different type of meal.

Roast Country Pigeon

As a little kid growing up when things were a bit tough, I can remember Mum cooking up batches of these birds with gravy and bread sauce. There was usually a bit left over for tomorrow.

Ingredients

Pigeons or other small birds
Big dob of margarine per bird
Salt and pepper to taste
Splash of cooking oil
Handful of plain flour
1 pannikin of milk
1 pannikin of breadcrumbs
1 small onion

How to do it

Take the birds and pluck, gut, clean and wash well. Wipe the birds dry. Season them inside with pepper and salt and put a big dob of margarine inside each—this makes them moist.

Throw a good splash of cooking oil in the hot camp oven, put birds in and baste well while they are cooking. Takes about half an hour or so.

GRAVY: Drain off some of the oil from the camp oven and sprinkle in some flour and brown slightly. Add a little water, stir well till it boils.

BREAD SAUCE: In a saucepan cook the whole small onion in the milk until onion is soft. Put breadcrumbs to soak in the milk. Beat up onion and breadcrumbs with a fork, add a good pinch of salt, and let boil.

Serve birds with the gravy poured over and with the bread sauce on the side. Eat with roast spuds for an unreal meal.

Camp Oven Quail

There are many ways of cooking these little birds, but to most country folk this one is possibly the most popular.

Ingredients

Quail (enough to go around)
Salt and pepper
Breadcrumbs
Margarine
Drops of lemon concentrate

How to do it

First catch the quail. Pluck and clean the birds, making sure the tail is removed. Inside each bird put one spoonful of breadcrumbs well seasoned with salt and pepper, and a small lump of margarine. Put the birds into a hot greased camp oven, and occasionally spoon juices over until cooked.

When cooked, put each bird on a piece of hot margarine-covered toast, and pour over a spoonful of juice. Serve with lemon drops and vegies.

They're that good they will even make you "tweet".

Black and White goose

The tropical parts of Australia are where you find these handsome looking birds. They can be a bit "gamey" but, with some good care and preparation they can be a terrific feed. There is a couple of ways of cooking them. Try this way for a change. Magpie geese are a protected species. Check with your local dept to find out when the season is open.

Ingredients

1 bird

2 pannikins of water

3 or 4 pinch's of cayenne pepper

3 or 4 rashers of bacon

2 chicken stock cubes

4 slices of bread

Salt and pepper

Some oil

Two small onions

5 pannikins of milk

How to do it

Pluck, clean and remove the tail section of the bird, pour the milk into a sealer bag or a clean bucket, place the bird into the milk, cover completely and let soak for a few hours or overnight (keep cool). In a bowl break up the bread, add cayenne pepper, half a diced onion, a pinch of salt and a few drops of milk, mix until a smooth pulp is formed. Stuff the bird and rub with salt put the bird into a lightly greased camp oven, cover the bird with the bacon rashers and onion rings. Dissolve the stock cubes in water, add to the camp oven. Place camp oven into coals and cook for a couple of hours, check and taste for seasoning, adjust if necessary. When cooked Serve with boiled beans and spuds.

FAST BAKE SPUDS

When baking spuds stick a metal skewer through the spud. They cook quicker.

Long Legs and Flat Feet

I love the serene beauty of Australia, sitting under a gumtree and doing nothing. The only noise you can here is a happy sounds of the birds busily doing their daily chores. If you're lucky you may see a couple of emu's pecking at the seed on the ground or watching a mob of kangaroos enjoying their daily intake of tucker. This is where they belong, out in the wild, free to do as they wish. The good thing about our Australian wild life is, we can still enjoy their tantalising tastes by specialised breeding and farming of these creatures which will ensure their survival. Do the right thing buy your meat from a butchers who specialise in these products.

Ingredients

Emu meat (preferably the breast, available from selected butchers)

Cooking oil

2 pannikins of milk

3 slices of bread

Small onion

Salt and pepper

Some spuds & pumpkin

Half pannikin of flour

Some shakes of mixed herbs

How to do it

Pour the milk into a sealer bag or a bowl, place in the emu breast, cover completely and put into an esky, let soak for a few hours or over night. To make the stuffing. In a bowl, break up the bread, add half a diced onion, a few shakes of salt and pepper, a couple of shakes of mixed herbs add a splash or 2 of milk, mix well until a pulp is formed.

Remove meat from milk and dry. On a flat board and using a beer bottle, roll meat flat, spoon stuffing over meat, roll up and tie of with fine wire. Rub salt over the roll and drizzle cooking oil over. In a hot camp oven, drop in a slurp of cooking oil, place in the roll, roast for a good hour, turn the meat. Add spuds and pumpkins, turning occasionally, when cooked remove and keep warm. Put in some flour and a dash or water; stir to make a gravy out of the juices. When cooked carve and serve.

Meat — Mild & Game

Bull Slabs

This is my older brother's favourite way to cook a lump of steak. His nickname is Slab and the steak came off a bull so hence its name, Bull Slab.

Ingredients

1 lump of steak (old)
Vegemite
1/2 packet French onion soup
Some foil

How to do it

First of all get your camp oven hot. Smear Vegemite lightly on both sides of the steak.

Make an envelope out of the foil and put the steak into it. Sprinkle the French onion soup over the steak. Close the envelope completely on all sides—this ensures that no juices escape out of the envelope.

Put the envelope into the camp oven and cook for, say, 25 minutes with coals on the lid.

When it's cooked the way you want it, serve with *Bell Spuds* for a fantastic meal that would make any pub cook envious.

Bully Buttock

Put 'er on early, go fishin' for the arvo. When you come back ravenous, she'll be done.

Ingredients

1 kilo rump steak
2 good spoonfuls of margarine and cooking oil
3 beef stock cubes
2 pannikins of water
1/2 pannikin of tomato sauce
12 small onions (whole)
5 rashers of chopped bacon
12 small peeled potatoes
1 packet of dry peas
Some flour

How to do it

Get your camp oven hot then put in margarine and cooking oil. Chop steak into 1-inch bits and roll in flour. Put into the camp oven and brown. Then add chopped bacon, water, and the rest of the ingredients. Cook *slowly* for 3–4 hours.

When cooked serve with *Aussie Damper*. It's great, mate.

Onions without tears

When peeling onions cut the bottom (root part) first and peel up. Don't cut the top until you've finished peeling. This will help keep the tears away.

Steaming Roo

This is really different, the steaming roo, sounds interesting takes half a day or more to cook, looks not to bad, smells great and has fantastic flavours.

Ingredients

Roo steak (from most specialised butchers) or any other meat

1 steamer or boiler or a good sized tin with a sealed lid or an earthenware jar with a tight-fitting lid

Bacon rashers	**3 onions**	**1/3 pannikin sauce**
Plenty of boiling water	**Some salt**	**Plenty of pepper**

Quite a few splashes of red wine

How to do it

Cut the steaks about 10 mm thick and about 100 mm. long, peel and slice the onions into rings. Lay two bacon rashers flat on the bottom of your boiler, put a steak on top, then the onions and plenty of pepper and a pinch of salt, then add more bacon, meat and onions and so on; keep repeating until all is used. Cover the lot with a cloth and seal the lid, put the boiler into the camp oven or saucepan or a tin bucket half full of boiling water and let it steam for a good half day. Keep topping up the saucepan with boiling water. At about the two-hour mark, pour in the sauce; about half an hour later pour in the wine and let it finish cooking.

Serve with scones or toast you may be surprised.

Raging Steer

In the dog house, things not going your way, being yelled at, drinking too much and playing up? I can relate to most of these things; after all, you're on holiday. You have to cheer her up, take her fishing for the arvo. When you get back to camp spoil her, cook her a fair dinkum six-star meal. Here's a way of doing it; after all, if I can cook it anybody can.

Ingredients (per person)

- 1 spud about 75mm across
- 1 onion
- Grated cheese
- Tomato sauce
- Some water
- 1 nice piece of steak
- 1 egg yolk
- Salt and pepper
- 2 or 3 drops of Tabasco sauce
- Butter or margarine

How to do it

In a saucepan pour in a small pannikin of salted water, add a spoonful of butter, bring to the boil, cut a slab about 10 mm thick out of the centre of the spud. Put into a saucepan and cook, turning now and then until golden brown; don't replace water if it evaporates.

Heat a frying pan and melt in some butter, place in steak, seal and turn, add salt and pepper, cook to your liking. Remove and rest. Finely dice 1/3 of the onion, place in a bowl, add cheese, 1 egg yolk, salt and pepper and mix well.

Have your camp oven hot, place in cooked steak, put the onion cheese and egg mix on top, cook until cheese melts and egg cooks.

Make the sauce, cut the remaining onion into rings, and put into the frying pan. Add a few good slurps of tomato sauce, plus a few drops of Tabasco sauce and stir. Cook until onions are soft.

To serve, place spud on the bottom of the plate put the steak and topping on the spud, pour the sauce mixture around the food and place a sprig of parsley (if any) or a gum leaf on the top. This is campfire cooking, six-star style in the bush.

She will enjoy it and you will be back in favour — perhaps!

Rough but Honest

The old swaggies used to cook this way, that is, if they had some meat then all they needed was a fire. This doesn't look much, tastes fair is easy to do and will keep you going.

Ingredients

A big bit of steak
A spoonful of dripping
A bit of chook wire
A couple of pinches of Salt & Pepper
Tomato, Worcestershire, and barbecue sauce

How to do it

If you only have one fire, the one to keep you warm, let it burn down to a nice bed of coals, carefully lay your chook wire over the coals so it won't collapse. Mix the dripping, salt and pepper and whatever sauce you have; if you ain't got no sauce don't worry. Rub the mixture over the steak, lay the steak on the chook wire and let it cook. Then turn, keeping a close eye on the coals; if they need a stir up, well stir em up. When done to your liking serve, with coal-roasted spuds. It's rough but honest.

Stump Meat

You don't have to be a master chef to knock this one up. And another good thing about it is there ain't many dishes or cleaning-up to do. This is my kind of meal.

Ingredients

1 good lump of steak approx. 1 kg
1 packet of soup—e.g. French onion
1/2 pannikin of water

How to do it

Cut steaks into bits and chuck into a hot camp oven. Sprinkle steak with soup mix. Pour in water and put the lid on the camp oven, not forgetting to put some hot coals on the lid.

Cook for about 1 1/2 hours, but you've got to keep checking on it. Serve with the sauce poured over, and with *Vegie Kebabs*.

NT steaks, eggs, onions

If you're on a trip up north or live there and have a chance to procure some buffalo steak, then try this out.

Ingredients

Buffalo steaks

2 eggs

Margarine

4 large onions (cut into rings)

Salt and pepper

Worcestershire, tobasco and tomato sauce

How to do it

Get your pan or hot plate hot, melt some margarine and start frying the onion. Mix salt, pepper and sauces together to make a baste. Put the steak into the pan. Sear one side then turn and spread the baste, let fry for a few minutes then turn and spread more of the baste and let it fry for another few minutes, meanwhile don't let the onion burn.

When the steak is nearly done to you liking, break in the eggs and fry in the steak juices.

FAT — GETTING IT RIGHT

To get the right temperature of the fat, a blue fume will be rising. To test, drop in a piece of bread, it should brown very quickly.

'Roo Tender Loin

This is the go—the fair-dinkum Aussie-bred feed. No muckin' around. Just real good old-fashioned tucker at its best.

Ingredients

A big lump of kangaroo steak or enough to go around
Some cooking oil (preferably good stuff)
Salt and pepper

How to do it

Get your kangaroo steak, if you can find some, and marinate it in the cooking oil for about half a day, or longer, or until you get around to it. In the meantime get some vegies ready.

Heat your pan by hanging it over the fire, then chuck your steak in the pan with some salt and pepper and slowly cook him up, turning him as necessary. When he's cooked he's done.

Now sit back, look at the stars, and enjoy a fair-dinkum meal of meat and vegies while living in the land of the Southern Cross.

Meat dried out

Never pierce the meat while cooking, this lets out all the juices. When turning your meat, use a lifter or a knife and spoon, or stick a fork into the fat.

Jolly Jumbucks

Either at home or away, I don't reckon you can beat a good feed of chops, especially with this ripper sauce over them.

Ingredients

8 chops
2 onions
Salt and pepper
1/3 pannikin of tomato sauce
2 spoons of Worcestershire sauce
A few shakes of garlic
Good spoon of flour
Small spoonful of sugar

How to do it

Cut off the excess fat from the chops and cook in a hot frypan until nearly done. Mix all other ingredients with a little water and pour over the chops. Cook until the mixture thickens.

Serve with spuds and beans.

Desert Chops

Egypt 1964, I was wandering through the desert between Port Said and Suez, through the heat haze I spotted a few camels and some blokes dressed in robes standing around in the blazing sun. I wandered over and said g'day and asked them what they were doing. In sign language they told me they were cooking goat for their dinner. The aroma coming out of the sand was fantastic. They scraped away the sand and pulled out an old beaten up earthenware pot. The amazing thing was, that there were only a few warm rocks to cook on plus the heat of the sand. They lifted the lid, the stuff inside looked horrible, smelt fantastic and tasted sought of alright. This meal is similar to the way they done it.

Ingredients

7 or 8 goat chops
2 large onions
Big dollop of margarine
3 stock cubes
3 big spoonfuls curry powder
Salt & pepper
2 spoonfuls of flour
2 pannikins boling water
2 spoonfuls of jam
12 drops lemon juice
Some wine

How to do it

Over there they cook in earthenware pots; we have not got one of those, we will use a camp oven, melt in some margarine, cut the chops into pieces, put into the camp oven with the quartered onions, cook until brown, remove, drain camp oven. Mix the curry, jam, flour, lemon juice, salt and pepper to taste, crumble in stock cubes, add boiling water and wine. Return meat and onions to the camp oven and give it a good stir.

Bury camp oven into coals and let simmer for 3 hours depending on the fire, lift lid and test for flavour and adjust if necessary. Put lid back on, let simmer until you're happy.

Serve straight from the pot with damper and have a happy Arab-Aussie day.

Scottish Venison

You take the high road and I'll take the low road. I took the high road to the highlands of north Scotland a long time ago and met a wonderful old Scotsman, who was of all things a camp cook. "Laddie," he said, "would you like to try some wee venison?" "Yes, sir," I said.

As he was cooking the meal he was trying to explain what he was doing. His accent was so broad, I couldn't understand, so he wrote down this recipe and said, "Now, laddie, you take this recipe to Orrstralia and cook it for all the laddies and lassies".

Ingredients

Shoulder of venison

Few good dollops of dripping

Couple pannikins of beef stock

Few shakes of black pepper

Few good shakes of all spice

Pannikin of red wine

How he done it

Hang the venison until tender, take out the bone, lay meat on flat board and roll out with a beer bottle until it's flat, spread some dripping, a few shakes of pepper and a few shakes of all spice. Roll the meat up and tie securely with butcher's string.

Put into a Bedourie oven together with the bones, the stock, a few more shakes of pepper and the wine. Put the lid on and place the oven on top of the coals and let it stew and simmer for half a day, check now and then, when tender, its done.

Serve, cut the roll into 1 inch slices, place on a warm plate and pour gravy over. To enhance this Scottish meal, add some freshly cooked vegies. When eating, please wear your kilt and keep your sporran under control.

Drovers' Stew

Drovers and boundary riders are nearly a thing of the past. My good mate "Griffo" in his younger days was a boundary rider and a real handy rodeo rider. He was an absolute superstar in the boxing ring, undefeated for 3 years in his weight division. Instead of being a pro boxer Griffo ended up as a master butcher and a great camp cook. Here is one of his recipes and it's fantastic.

Ingredients

A couple of handfuls of 1-in. square chuck steak or roo meat

4 or 5 medium spuds chopped small

1 teaspoon cooking salt

Enough water to twice cover meat

2 or 3 onions chopped into 4 pieces

1 sliced carrot

How to do it

Cut meat into 1-inch squares, cut half the amount of spuds into small pieces. Put the meat and spuds into a bucket. Add enough water to twice cover the meat, add the salt, cover and let stand overnight.

Next day, heat camp oven, pour contents of bucket into the camp oven, bring to the boil and simmer for a good hour or so, lift the lid and add the remaining spuds, onions and carrots. Return the lid and cook until the vegies are cooked and the juices reduced to gravy.

If you wish to have dumplings in your stew, add them when you put the last vegies in.

Serve hot today or better still, warm up for tomorrow.

FAT — HOT

If you're going to fry anything, make sure the fat is hot, real hot. This seals the outside of the food straight away, and stops the juices from getting out, and keeps the fat from getting in. But be careful, hot fat is dangerous, and it can burst into flames.

Battler's Tucker

If you're way out in the bush, miles from anywhere, maybe you're fencing or cutting wood, perhaps doing a spot of fishing and your tucker box is getting low, the fish won't jump onto the end of your line and your meat supply is exhausted. You feel like a decent feed, this is the one for you. It's easy to do, doesn't cost much and will fill up that hollow spot.

Ingredients

1 tin of camp pie

2 or 3 spuds

1 egg

1 onion

2 ripe tomatoes

Some salt and pepper

A dash or 2 of milk

How to do it

Peel and cut the spuds into small pieces, place into a billy or saucepan and cover with water, add a pinch or two of salt, bring to the boil then simmer until a fork pierces spuds easily.

Drain water off; add a few good shakes of pepper and a good dollop of margarine and a dash or two of milk, mash it until it is smooth. Finely chop the onion and tomatoes, remove camp pie from tin and place into a bowl, add the egg and mix well.

Press mixture into a small camp oven, top with a thick covering of the mashed spuds. Place camp oven into the coals and let it cook moderately for nearly an hour. When cooked serve straight away with sauce.

It's better then eating nothing.

A Real Different Meal
If You're Daring

Achilles Eel

Eels are slippery little beggars that love nothing better than catching a mug on the end of a rod and doing their damnedest to drag him into the creek or river. As this recipe is about how to cook, not how to catch, land, handle or outwit the slimy creatures we'll just say that having done so, and by following the direction below, you'll be rewarded with its tantalising taste.

Ingredients

A couple of eels
1 pannikin of plain flour
A couple of pinches of salt
A couple of pinches of pepper
1/2 pannikin of cooking oil

How to do it

Who won the fight? I bet he gave you a hard time. Now that you have him, first of all get the axe and chop his head off. Skin, gut and rinse him well and slice into pieces. Put the pieces into boiling water and let the pieces boil with the lid on for 15 minutes, remove slices and let them cool.

On a flat board mix the salt pepper and flour and roll the slices of eel in the dry mixture. Heat your hot plate or pan and drop in some cooking oil, gently put the floured slices in and fry until brown, turning every now and then.

Coat-of-arms Stew

What about this for an idea? Next Australia day long weekend, pack up the trailer with your camping gear, load up the family and head off to your favourite camping site

Set yourself up, have a good fire going and when Australia day comes impress the family by cooking them a fair dinkum Aussie meal.

Ingredients

Equal parts of kangaroo and emu meat (about 1 kilo, available from specialist butchers)

2 onions

2 vegetable stock cubes

Some salt

1 small pannikin of red wine

A few shakes of cooking oil

A few good shakes of garlic granules

1 parsnip, carrot, zucchini and Swede

1 stick of celery

Half pannikin of water

Some corn flour

How to do it

Have your camp oven warm, splash in some cooking oil, cut the meat into 25mm squares, remove any fat, peel and dice the onions, chuck into the camp oven and give it a stir, add the crumbed stock cubes, some salt, the red wine and water, stir again, let simmer for 2 hours.

Peel and chop the parsnip, carrot, swede and celery, add to the stew, slice the unpeeled zucchini and add, stir again, let cook for a further 1.5 hours, check for seasoning, and adjust if necessary. If the gravy is to thin stir in some corn flour.

When done serve with a freshly cooked damper, wash down with billy tea and have a happy Australia Day.

Billabong Croc

If you see one of these big fellers having a doze in the sun, beware; he's probably foxing. Don't try to put salt on his tail; if you do, he may give you the crocodile roll. In other words, let him have his billabong. Hey, these fellars have a nasty disposition. I reckon they have a couple of packets of angry pills for breakfast, then try and get some mug human for tea.

Ingredients

Some croc steaks (available from selected butcher)

Small spoonful of lemon juices

A slurp of soy sauce

Some mushrooms

Good splashes of cooking oil

A good slurp of rum

1 onion and some salt

How to do it

To make the marinade, in a bowl, mix the oil, lemon juice, soy and rum. Cut the croc steaks into 25mm squares, put into the mixture, let soak for about 30 minutes. Peel the onions, clean the mushrooms and cut both into same size squares as the meat. Remove croc pieces from marinade, thread onto a skewer with the onion and mushrooms pieces. Have your hot plate or pan hot, place in filled skewer turning occasionally, brushing over with marinade until done.

Serve with some hot buttered scones for a different smoky taste.

FAT — NOT HOT ENOUGH

If you put the food in before the fat is hot, it will be greasy and spongy and horrible and give you the burps.

Kai Time

Most of the world's top cooks and chefs carve out a career working in the best hotels and restaurants in London, Paris and New York. Not our Hori, he was taught by his grandfather, who lived on a tiny island in the Pacific Ocean, Chatham Island. Hori doesn't need a stainless steel oven or a big white hat; he only needs some fresh food, a shovel and a fire to prepare native "kai".

Ingredients

Lump of meat, chook, fish, unpeeled spuds, pumpkin, carrots, a whole cabbage with stalk removed, peeled onions, foil, clean chook wire, 2 cotton wet tea towels, 3 or 4 wet hession bags, a couple of gallons of water, some old steel parts Eg: brake drums, axe heads or volcanic rocks (most rocks explode when hot, so take care, hot steel parts are safer).

How to do it (Hori style)

Dig a pit 1metre square x 750mm deep, set up fire in the pit, put rocks and steel on top of the wood, then ignite. Build the fire until it fills the pit; it will take about 3 hours. Make a wire basket out of the chook wire to comfortably fit the pit, place meat in bottom of basket, foil wrap fish & chook and place on top of meat, foil wrap, all vegies and stuffing, fill the cabbage core with margarine, wrap in foil, place all vegies on top of fish and chooks. Cover top of food only with a couple of wet cotton tea towels, saturate 3 or 4 spud bags in clean drinking water.

Fire is now burnt down and the steel is red hot, clear pit of everything and clean out ash and coals. Replace red hot steel & rock evenly, place basket on top, put wet spud bags over the basket, and make sure all is completely covered (important).

Gently back fill with soil until steam is not escaping, if any leaks plug, wait for 3 hours, gently uncover the pit

Serve with a gravox mix, apple sauce or just plain sauce.

Witjuti Grubs

You beauty—have a go at these. All the old fair-dinkum Aussies have been eatin' 'em for years, and now you can get 'em in a restaurant, so why not try 'em for yourself while out in the bush?

How to catch him

To catch a witjuti, you will probably find him in any number of trees, but wattle is his favourite haunt. If you see a tree with a hole in its trunk and some evidence of sawdust around I reckon you've hit the jackpot. Now to get him out you can use a bit of thin wire or an old inner speedo cable and put a sharp point on the end with a file. Bend the wire around to make a type of a barb, shove the wire into the hole and turn around a few times, and then with luck when you pull it out you could have a grub hanging on the end.

How to eat him raw

This'll get the sheilas going. Hold his head with the finger and thumb of your left hand and grab his skin near his anus with your other hand and pull out his entire innards. Close your eyes and bite off his body behind his head. Now you mightn't like the sound of this, but the witjuti is one of the tastiest and most nutritious foods around. The grub is sort of a cream colour, and it grows to about 4 or 5 inches long.

How to cook him

Throw him complete into the hot ashes for a couple of minutes, then gut him and eat him. Or put him into a hot pan with a bit of margarine. But don't cook him for too long.

Well witjuti grubs are great, so don't worry. They only eat wood and are probably the cleanest bush food in the country.

The Old Snags & Mince

Bloodied Dogs

This is no "yapping" matter, this is a fair dinkum country way of making the old snags taste a bit better than beaut.

Ingredients

12 sausages
1 pannikin of mashed potatoes
2 tomatoes (pulp)
1 egg
1 egg yolk
Pepper and salt to taste
Some breadcrumbs
Cooking oil

How to do it

Rip the sausage meat out of the skins and put with potato, tomato pulp, pepper and salt to taste. Work it in with a well-beaten egg yolk. Turn the mixture into sausage shapes and roll in egg and breadcrumbs.

Have your pan hot and chuck in some cooking oil and sausage shapes and fry until cooked. You have to turn them over a few times to get them cooked properly.

Serve with plenty of sauce.

Ironbark snags

The bloke who created this way of knocking up a feed of curried snags in a camp oven is an amazing fella. A jack of all trades, musician, superb horseman and supplier of working horses and cattle to the movie industry. He is also the owner-operator of a trail horse riding and bush cabin holiday retreat business on the outskirts of Bendigo.

Dusty as he is known to his mates is also a great camp oven cook. I went to see him one Thursday afternoon we had a yarn for a while, he then suggested that I join him and about 20 other blokes for tea.

He opened the door of his huge wood fired oven and lifted out 2 camp ovens, one filled to the brim with his famous curried snags, the other one had a superb looking damper.

All the freeloaders hoed in like a mob of unfed mongrel dogs and of course we had a few drinks to finish off the night.

I said to him, "Mate, the snags were great, can I have the recipe?" He said, "If you stop twisting my arm, I'll write it out for you".

Ingredients

8 or 9 snags
2 carrots
4 spuds
1 orange
2 onions
2 pkt chicken noodle soup
3 big spoons of curry powder
Some water and slurps of rum
1 big spoonful of gravox

How to do it

Cut the snags into bits, peel and dice the onions, spuds and orange, slice the carrots, chuck the lot into the camp oven, add the chicken noodle soup, curry and the gravox, completely cover with water, add a couple of good splashes of rum, give the mixture a stir, put the camp oven into the coals and simmer, every now and then give it a stir and cook until the carrots are soft.

Serve with a lump of freshly cooked damper and wash down with a good Aussie rum.

Toad-in-the-Hole

This'll get the "croak" out of ya and put some hop back into ya. Cook it and eat it just before dark and then go and check the fishin' lines. If it's misty it could give you a "frog" in the throat.

Ingredients

1 pannikin of self-raising flour
1 egg
1/2 pint of milk
Half-a-dozen sausages
2 good spoons of margarine
Some salt

How to do it

Mix up a batter with the flour, salt, egg and milk the same as you would for pancakes.

Get your hot camp oven and put in the margarine. Pour in the batter. Drop in the sausages and face them in one direction, put the lid on and let them bake for about half an hour.

Eat 'em with some spuds and tomatoes.

EUCY TO THE RESCUE

COLDS: put a couple of drops of eucalyptus oil on a handkerchief or a piece of rag and breathe in every now and then.

PULLED MUSCLE: get one part of eucalyptus oil to three parts of oil and rub it in. It works.

STINGS: also good rubbed on stings, diluted or undiluted.

Balls And Mushies

Years ago when off camping, most folk would only take a frypan, some salt and a bucket of fat and live off the land. But things have changed. There are more people out in the bush and so naturally most people are taking their food with them. This meal is the ideal holiday tucker, easy to prepare, and goes down pretty good.

Ingredients

2 pannikins of mince steak
1 onion
1 carrot
2 good shakes of garlic granules
1 beaten egg
1/4 pannikin of plain flour
1 good spoonful of margarine
1 small spoonful of cooking flour
Mushroom Sauce

How to do it

Chop onions and carrot very finely. Combine with mince, garlic and egg and mix well. Make into balls.

Roll balls in flour and flatten into a hot oiled frypan and cook, occasionally turning.

When cooked, remove rissoles and keep hot while preparing *Mushroom Sauce*.

Roo & Damper

Stone the crows, starve the lizards, fair dinkum mate this is Aussie tucker at its best. I'll lay you eggs to youngens you'll have a crack at this and then say "bloody bewdy mate".

Ingredients

2 pannikins of roo mince

2 eggs

Breadcrumbs

Salt and pepper

3 onions

2 good shakes of mixed herbs

Some flour

Some cheese

Scrub relish

1 warm fresh damper

Some margarine

How to do it

Dice one onion fine, cut the other 2 onions into rings, beat the eggs. On a seasoned floured board, mix roo meat breadcrumbs, diced onion, eggs and mixed herbs, roll into good sized balls. In a heated pan, melt in margarine, add onion rings, the balls and press flat. Fry until brown on bottom then turn, when nearly cooked add cheese to the top of the meat and leave until the cheese is melted.

Cut your warm damper into decent slabs, spread with margarine, put roo meat on top, cover with onion rings and smother with scrub relish.

Brew up some billy tea and the stare skywards & see if you can find the Southern Cross. I told ya, bloody bewdy mate!

Meat Loaf and Fried Damper

Sitting by the river, no fish to be found
The rabbits have gone quiet and there's no quail around
Instead of sitting here better go back to the camper
For tea tonight it's Meat Loaf and Fried Damper.

Ingredients

Half a kilo of mince steak
Half a kilo of sausage mince
1 diced onion
Handful of flour
1 egg
Good pinch of salt
Good pinch of pepper

How to do it

Dice the onion finely and mix together with both meats. Break the egg into the meat and mix thoroughly.

Shape into a loaf and roll in flour. Place in an oiled camp oven and cook for 2 hours.

When Meat Loaf is cooked, remove from camp oven and keep warm. Now cook your *FRIED DAMPER*.

Serve Meat Loaf and Fried Damper with roast spuds. Have a delicious meal.

Mince Parcels In Foil

This is bush tucker at its best. You can either get 'em ready at home or get 'em up by the fire, either way you do it you are in for a real treat as they are tops.

Ingredients

2 handfuls of mince (or sausage meat)
3 onions
Some garlic granules
1 packet of dried peas
Half-a-handful of carrots
3 spuds
A good pinch of salt
Some Worcestershire sauce

How to do it

Mix all ingredients together then break into easily handled portions, say four or five. Wrap in foil, and chuck into the coals. Cook for approximately 30 to 45 minutes.

These parcels can be made with almost anything that is around, and can be done at home and kept in the Esky. For different meats try bacon, celery, cheese and corn.

Serve with *Mick's Spuds* for a real different meal.

Mushies & Vegies

Keep the green in the bean

A bit of carb soda in beans and peas while they're cooking gives them a good green colour.

Midnight Mushies

This is the perfect midnight snack just before hitting the hay, they only take a few minutes to make.

Ingredients

Large mushrooms (enough to go around)
Worcestershire sauce
Bacon rashers

How to do it

Chop bacon and cook in a hot frypan. Spoon bacon into mushroom caps and sprinkle Worcestershire sauce liberally over the top. Cook in the camp oven until mushrooms are well heated through.

My mouth's watering now.

WARNING

Field mushrooms are identified by the white ring around the stem, and pink gills—which darken on maturity.

NOT TO BE CONFUSED with yellow-staining mushrooms which, when scratched on the caps or stem with fingernail or knife turn yellow, and which also have a strong ammonia smell if cooked. THROW AWAY AS THEY ARE POISONOUS.

Pan-fried Mushies

If you happen onto a paddock of fresh mushies, or you've bought some from the greengrocer, here is an easy way of cooking them.

Ingredients

Fresh mushrooms (enough to go around)
Big dob of margarine
Salt and pepper
Some flour

How to do it

Peel, clean and slice the mushrooms while your frypan is getting hot. Then pop in the margarine and the mushroom slices. Sprinkle with salt and pepper and cook for a few minutes, turning occasionally.

If a gravy is desired, add a little flour and stir.

Delicious on damper dripping with margarine, or served over meat.

Vegie Kebabs

Before you leave home make these things up and put them in a bag in the esky. Then when you get to where you are going, get your fire started and put these on to start cooking. Unload the ute, and when you've finished that, these kebabs should be ready to turn over.

Ingredients

Fresh vegies
Some salt
Wire skewers

How to do it

Cut vegies to the size you reckon is about right, then thread onto skewers. Cook over a medium fire turning now and then. Don't forget, you want your vegies hot and not mushy. Add salt to taste. Good with bread and butter.

Ernie's Vegies

No pan, no camp oven, all you need is a good bed of coals, some veggies and a wet hessian bag; this is Ernie's way.

Ingredientsg

1 good-sized spud
1 lump of pumpkin
1 onion
1 parsnip or carrot
1 wet hessian bag or wet bark

How to do it

Rub salt all the over the vegies, wrap them in the wet hessian bag, or wet bark, nice tight. Dig a hole under your main fire put some red hot coals in. Place the bag on top of the coals; back fill the hole with coals and dirt. Let them steam until easily pierced with a fork. When ready, remove, clean up vegies and serve.

Spuds

Bell Spuds

This is a concoction of a recipe that's used every day in classy restaurants and pubs, and is easily converted to a camp oven to give you a classy side-dish to your main meal. The name happened to be on some paper recipes I got one day.

Ingredients

Some spuds (enough to go around)
A couple of big onions
Salt and pepper
Some garlic sprinkles
Half a pannikin of milk (or enough)
Some cheese slices
Some margarine

How to do it

Grease your camp oven and get it hot. Then peel and cut the onions into rings and put into the bottom of the camp oven. Peel, wash and slice the spuds into about 1/4-inch-thick slices and place over the onions. Give 'em some salt and pepper, and a fine sprinkle of garlic. Chuck in the milk and cover with sliced cheese.

Put the camp oven in the coals, with some coals on the lid, and cook. Should take about 30 minutes or so, but check. When they pierce easily with a fork, they're done.

Serve with *Bull Slabs*. This will be one of the most gourmet meals you will ever cook in the bush.

Bullocky Bread

Cop a loaf of this. No yeast, only bits and pieces out of your tuckerbox. And if I can eat it you can.

Ingredients

2 spuds
1 pannikin of water
1 pannikin of self-raising flour
Pinch of salt

How to do it

Peel and boil the spuds in a saucepan and then mash them in their own water and let go cold. Add self-raising flour and salt then mix—an ice cream container is ideal for this.

Knead well—you should know how to do this by now—and shape like a damper. Grease sides and bottom of the camp oven and put in damper. Bake for about 30 minutes.

Use the "knocking" test to see if it's cooked. When it sounds hollow he's done.

NO-SPLASH BOILING

When boiling peas or beans add a small bit of margarine to the water, they reckon it stops it from boiling over.

Dydi's Savoury Spud Cakes

If you have had a bad day's fishing, and if you're starving hungry, here's a meal that's quick 'n' easy and will pacify that rumbling stomach.

Ingredients

6 large potatoes
1/2 pannikin of flour
2 medium onions
A couple of eggs
4 slices of bacon
4 spoonfuls of margarine

How to do it

Take the potatoes, peel, boil in water until cooked—when easily pierced by fork. Mash with margarine, salt and pepper. Add the rest of the ingredients and mix well.

Hang pan over the coals and heat, melt in a couple of spoonfuls of margarine, and spoon in dobs of mixture. Cook until brown, then turn.

Serve hot with salt, pepper and plenty of sauce.

Mick's Spuds

This is how the old timers used to cook their spuds. It's original and believe me it works. Just ask Mick if you're ever up Deni. way.

Ingredients

2 spuds per person

How to do it

Scoop a hole in the bottom of the coals and chuck in the spuds and cover with dirt and coals and let 'em cook on their own. After 20 minutes or so check by piercing with a knife.

When cooked, serve with rabbit or fish or any other meal.

Mock Fish

It's not fair-dinkum fish, but if you can't catch one or go to the shop and buy one, this'll have to do.

Ingredients

To each person you are cooking for:
2 good-size spuds
1 egg
1 onion
Salt and pepper
Cooking oil

How to do it

Peel and grate the spuds and the onion, then squeeze out the juices. Add egg and a good pinch of salt and pepper. Mix well. Chuck into a hot frypan with cooking oil. Fry, turning occasionally, until golden brown.

Serve with plenty of sauce.

Coal-roasted Spuds in Foil

There are many ways and combinations of cooking spuds in the coals. This is the way we do it, and for years it has been successful. Why don't you try out your own combinations?

Ingredients

Some medium sized spuds enough to go around some foil

French onion soup mix

Margarine

Pepper

How to do it

Slice the spuds in half, don't cut all the way through, gently open the cut and put in a liberal amount of margarine and sprinkle French onion soup mix as well as a shake of pepper. Roll up the filled spuds completely in foil.

Dig a hole into the hot coals and put the spud parcels in, cover the spuds with more coals. Don't forget to count the number of spuds you have put into the fire otherwise you might find the balance tomorrow. Cook until you can easily pierce them with a fork.

Serve with a roast or have with a vegie lunch.

Spud Pie

When you're stuck out in the bush, who said you can't make up some of the best meals around? This one is that good even the best of bushies come back for more.

Ingredients

4 spuds
1/2 pannikin of cheese (grated)
1 packet of soup mix
2 spoons of margarine
1 pannikin of milk

How to do it

Grease your hot camp oven. Slice the spuds and arrange layers of spuds and soup mix in camp oven. Heat milk and pour over. Cook in moderate coals for 40–45 minutes or until the spuds are cooked through.

Remove lid of the camp oven, add extra milk if necessary, and top with cheese and a bit of margarine. Bake for a further 10 minutes until the cheese melts.

Serve as a side-dish with fish or meat. Excellent with *Bidsey's Crumbed Wild Duck* or *Roasted Underground Mutton.*

Spud Balls

Feel like a quick easy snack, these balls will fill you up. They are easy to do and will keep you going until the next good feed comes along. You and your cooked balls — what a combination!

Ingredients

Pkt of instant spud mix

Salt and pepper to taste

1 small egg

1 beaten egg

Some flour

Breadcrumbs

Margarine

How to do it

Prepare the spud mix as per pkt. Beat a small egg into the prepared spud mix. Divide into 12 or so small sections and work into balls with your hands. Season with some flour, roll the balls in the flour, then roll into the beaten egg, then into the breadcrumbs.

Have your pan hot and melt in some margarine, put the balls in and let them cook. Roll them around in the pan for even cooking. For some extra added flavours, mix in some cheese and chopped parsley.

Serve straight away and smother with sauce.

Re-cooking Leftovers

Feathered Fish

So you had a big catch yesterday and couldn't eat it all last night. Why not have it for brekkie with some eggs.

Ingredients

3 eggs
2 good spoonfuls of cooked fish
1 good spoonful of milk
Salt and pepper to taste
2 good spoonfuls of margarine

How to do it

In a bowl beat the eggs and add milk, add salt and pepper to taste. Have your frypan hot and add margarine, and then the flaked cooked fish. Add beaten eggs and cook slowly, stirring continuously until mixture thickens.

When ready, pour onto hot toast and tuck in, and wash down with billy tea.

TYING WIRE FOR A TOW ROPE

If your vehicle gets bogged and you need some wire from a fence to help you out, there is only one knot to use and that's the old farmer's figure-8 knot. Easy to do and won't come undone.

Jaffles In Coals

My memory goes back well over 60 years and I can't ever remember not having or constantly using a jaffle iron, it is one of the most popular camping utensils ever developed.

Ingredients

Sliced bread
Margarine
Filling (suggestions below)
Salt and pepper

How to do it

The fillings and combinations you can use are endless; eggs & bacon, tinned spaghetti or baked beans, cheese & onion, chicken on the wing, red & yellow-turkey gobble and most of all left over stews the list is endless, all that is needed is imagination.
Spread 2 slices of bread with margarine & place the buttered side down on the opened jaffle iron, add your special mixture to the bread then lay the other piece of bread over the mixture with the buttered side facing up. Close & lock the jaffle & place into the hot coals. Let it cook for a couple of minutes then turn. Do this a couple of times then open & check, when it's golden brown on both side it done.
Serve immediately for a top snack.

Paddy's Fish Cakes

If you've had a good catch the day before and you're worried about keeping the fish fresh, why not cook them all up at once, then re-cook as needed? Here is a way of doing it.

Ingredients

Remains of any cold fish
To each kilo:
About 1/2 kilo of mashed spuds
1 big dob of margarine
2 eggs
Milk
Breadcrumbs
Big pinch of salt
Pinch of pepper
Cooking oil

How to do it

Hang your pan over the coals to get hot and add margarine. Then chuck in and mix together the coarsely broken-up fish, mashed spuds, yolk of one egg, salt, pepper and a bit of milk to moisten.

Stir for a few minutes then place onto a plate and let cool.

When cold, make into flat round cakes. Wipe over with egg, smother with breadcrumbs, and fry in hot cooking oil.

Serve with peas or beans.

Modern Swaggies' Leftovers

If you had to cook all your meat up at once because you needed the Esky for other vital materials, well don't throw the cooked meat away, re-cook it the next day.

Ingredients

Any leftover cold meat, sliced
1 onion
2 tomatoes sliced
Salt and pepper
1 egg
Handful of flour
Some milk

How to do it

Put the flour and salt in a bowl, break an egg into centre of flour and mix it up well. Then put the milk in and mix to make a nice smooth batter.

Have your frypan hot and greased. Place together sliced meat, onions, and tomatoes. Cover in batter mixture and fry until golden brown.

Serve with chipped spuds and peas.

Something To Sweeten You Up

Balls of Fire

When its smoko time, these little hot balls will warm you up.

Ingredients

1 tin or pannikin or 2 of dripping
1 tsp of baking powder
½ tsp of salt
2 pannikin of flour
½ pannikin of milk (or water)
1 empty & clean beer can

How to do it

In a bowl mix the flour, baking powder, milk & salt into a light dough & roll it out to about 1/2" thick.

Now the difficult bit, cut the top and bottom out of the beer can to use as a cutter.

With your new cutter cut the dough into perfect circles, put the dripping into a saucepan & get it smoking, add the circles to the boiling fat & cook until thier crisp.
Perfect for that smoko.

Bread & Butter Pudding

The good old bread and butter pudding, the old farmer's wife's favourite sweet, I reckon they could bash this together with their eyes closed & it would still be perfect.

Ingredients

A few slices of bread
Some jam
A pinch or 2 of cinnamon
A couple spoonfuls of butter or margarine
A pannikin of milk
Some sultanas if any

How to do it

Butter the bread & smother with the jam.
Lightly grease the camp oven with butter. Gently place in the bread & slowly add the milk, Build up the layers of bread & milk, but do not completely cover the bread, sprinkle the top with some cinnamon or sultanas.
Put the camp oven in the coals & let cook for about 1/2 an hour. Serve immediately.

Dolly Varden

This'll sweeten the missus up, especially if you're at the camp on your own. Knock this one up for when she comes back. Sit her down, make her a cup of tea and give her a bit of this cake, then tell her you are going fishing with the boys again next week. Ha! ha! fat chance.

Ingredients

1/2 pannikin of butter or margarine
1/4 pannikin of sugar
Couple of eggs
One-and-a-bit pannikins of self-raising flour
1/2 pannikin of milk

How to do it

Get your *TWELVE GALLON OVEN* hot with good coals.

Mix the margarine and sugar to a creamy smooth texture, use an ice cream container for this. Then put in the eggs and beat well. *Slowly* add the self-raising flour and the milk bit by bit—it should now look like a batter.

Pour mixture into your greased cake tin and bake in your drum oven. It should take about an hour or so, but keep a close eye on your fire.

When it's done, and if you have any, pour cream over the top.

When serving, you have to have it with billy tea.

Campers' Fritters

You don't have to be the sharpest tool in the shed to bash up a batch of these.
There is only one "but"; you'll have to be sharper than a razor blade to keep your mates' grubby maulers off 'em after they're cooked.

Ingredients

A couple of eggs
1 pannikin of milk
Pinch of salt
4 tbl spoons of corn flour
1/2 pannikin of cooking oil

How to do it

Beat up the eggs , mix all other bits together to make a smooth batter; have your fry pan hot and pour in the cooking oil- when nice and hot add in spoonfuls of the mixture and fry until crisp and brown, when done drain them on some paper. Serve - smother them with jam mmmmm.

FAT — WITHOUT SPLASH AND SPLATTER

A small sprinkle of salt put into hot fat will help stop splattering. And make sure there's no moisture in the pan, as this makes the fat splash and splatter. Always have the food as dry as possible.

Mug Of Muck

This'll fix you up, and settle down your rumbling tummy. Or if you've had a big main meal, you need a nice settling pudding to finish off your big day.

Ingredients

Some sugar, about a spoonful
Pinch of salt
A pannikin of self-raising flour
A good spoonful of margarine
Some mixed dried fruit

How to do it

First of all, get your camp oven full of water, and get it boiling and keep it boiling while you prepare your pannikin of self-raising flour.

Add to the flour the spoonful of sugar and a pinch of salt, then mix in the margarine and dried fruit to make a real good dry dough. Drop the mixture into the boiling water, and keep it on the boil for a good half hour or so for every pannikin of flour you use.

If you get side-tracked and it boils a bit too long, don't worry, it will be OK.

If you're real serious about this meal, and you have a cloth bag with you, you can put the dough into the bag to hold it together for cooking. Or you can put the raw dough into a greased billy which can then be boiled inside a larger billy.

Serve with *Golden Syrup Sauce*.

Outback Fritters

These pancakes are perfect for that after-main-meal sweet. Or if you're off fishing or hunting, put a few in your pocket for when you get a little hungry later.

Ingredients

1 pannikin of self-raising flour
1 small spoonful of sugar
1 egg
3/4 pannikin of milk
A big dob of margarine
Some apple slices

How to do it

Put flour and sugar into a bowl, break an egg into the centre and combine with milk until smooth. Stir in melted margarine, then add slices of apples.

Have your frypan hot and greased, then drop spoonfuls of the mixture into the pan. Make sure there is a slice of apple in each pancake. Cook until the top bubbles on each pancake, then turn and cook until golden brown.

Serve as a snack with margarine and sugar. Beautiful!

BANANAS AND APPLES GONE A FUNNY COLOUR

To stop the discolouring on bananas and apples, splash some lemon juice over the top of them.

Golden Gold Pikelets

When things are tough and you walk so far
No sign of rabbits or money in the jar
You pass a stranger, what a welcome sight
He's broke to, this could be the night

You can smell tucker cooking a way up yonder
Walk in quietly, he says, G'day old timer
Pull up a log, you're looking pretty cold
I've run out of sugar and my pan's getting old
These will warm you up, just grab'em by hand
It's the golden gold, cooked gently in the pan.

Ingredients

2 eggs
1/4 pannikin of sugar
1/4 pannikin of milk
1 & 1/4 pannikin of SR flour
1 good spoonful of butter or marg (melted)
1 spoonful of golden syrup(melted)
1 pinch of carb soda(if any)

How to do it

Warm a saucepan and melt the butter or margarine & golden syrup. In a bowl beat the eggs & add the milk; mixing all the time. Add the sugar, flour, carb soda & the melted butter and golden syrup until a smooth texture is obtained.

Have your frypan or hot plate hot & melt in a good spoonful of margarine; then gently drop in spoonfuls of the mixture & cook, when golden on the bottom turn, then serve.

What a feed before hitting the hay & dream about the real golden gold.

Twelve Gallon Bun

This ain't so sexy and it ain't gonna hurt
If your feelin' a bit pecky or perhaps a bit of skirt
You could open a can or just prop for a while
Just read on a bit and give us a smile
Start mixin' and stirrin', the drum's ready for work
It smells real good, don't drop it in the dirt
Slam a bun in the oven—Hey mate it sure works.

Ingredients

- 1/2 pannikin of mashed spuds
- Some sultanas
- 1/2 pannikin of sugar
- 1/2 pannikin of milk
- 1 pannikin of self-raising flour
- Bit of salt

How to do it

Chuck some real good coals into the bottom of your drum. Mix up all the ingredients and put into a cake tin, or something similar, but don't forget to smear it with some margarine first. Cook it for about 20 minutes. Keep a check on it and your fire, it is important.

When it's done and is still hot, smear the top with some margarine and sprinkle some sugar on it. Then hop into it.

Soaking The Meat & Sauces

Marinating

All the old cooks & swaggies never used to marinade anything. All they used to do was, rub the meat with salt & dripping and start cooking.
We have come along way since those "rugged" days & are now using things like herbs, sauces, spices & wines to enhance the flavour & tenderise our meats.
One of the most favoured methods of marinating meat & fish is simply wine. Another simple way of marinating meat is salty water & let it stand over night.
A simple way of marinating fish is lemon juice, salt & oil & even throw in some fresh herbs.
A couple of simple ways of marinating the delicate chicken, mix up some soy sauce & some wine or lemon juice, olive oil & garlic.
It is up to the individual to work out what flavours he or she needs. Here is another example, for meat, mix some onions, garlic, sauces, sea salt, black pepper & lemon juice. As you can see the list is endless & the marinating time can be from a few minutes to 24 hours. The big secret of marinating is to make sure the meat and fish are well coated & let soak at room temperature.
Next time you go bush, try out your own mixture & see what happens.

GOOD LUCK

MICE AND ANTS A PROBLEM

Get some mustard and vinegar and make into a paste. That'll get rid of them.

White Sauce

This recipe is quite adaptable and can be used for Steamed Fish and other tantalising meals you can bash up.

Ingredients

1 bit of margarine
2 spoonfuls of flour
Dash of milk
Splash of water
Pinch of salt

How to do it

Melt margarine into a pot or a saucepan and add flour. Stir well until smooth. Put in milk and water and give it a good stir until it's boiling.

Cook for 5–7 minutes and chuck in some salt to give it a good taste.

A different idea is to put in some grated cheese and stir until the cheese is melted.

Especially good served over *Steamed Fish*.

Bread Sauce

Ingredients

1 pannikin of milk
1 pannikin of breadcrumbs
1 small onion
Handful of plain flour

How to do it

In a saucepan cook the whole small onion in the milk until soft. Put in the breadcrumbs to soak. Beat up with a fork, add a good pinch of salt, and let boil.

Serve Bread Sauce on the side with *ROAST COUNTRY PIGEON* or other birds, and eat with roast spuds for an unreal meal.

Dead Horse Sauce

This is better than winning the Melbourne Cup at Flemington. Just throw it over your steak and let it ooze over and into the gravy. Then let your mates anguish over the look and taste. But if you want to, give 'em some. Be very reluctant.

Ingredients

1 small can of tomatoes
A couple of big spoons of oil
A good pinch of salt
A couple of good shakes of pepper
A couple of good shakes of garlic granules

How to do it

Make sure the tomatoes are bashed real fine, or to a pulp. Chuck the whole lot of ingredients into a saucepan or billy and cook it for about half an hour or so. You can give it a stir or two if you feel like it, don't let it burn.

Serve either hot or cold. There is enough Dead Horse here for you and three of your mates.

Golden Syrup Sauce

There's always one in the camp with a sweet tooth so sweeten her up. You never know, it could be the makings of a lovely friendship.

Ingredients

A couple of pannikins of water
2 spoonfuls of margarine
2 good spoonfuls of golden syrup

How to do it

Mix the ingredients together in the camp oven and bring to the boil. Simmer for 10 minutes.

Try simmering dumplings (*LEAD SINKERS* recipe) in the sauce and serving in a bowl with cream, if available. And see what happens.

Also serve with *MUG OF MUCK*, *PLOUGHMAN'S PIKELETS*, or the like.

GET RID OF THAT TOOTHACHE

Look straight ahead. Curve your fingers and with finger-tips press the point at the bottom of your cheekbone in a direct line from your pupil. Hold gently for one minute. If this doesn't work, go to the dentist and get it ripped out.

Mallee Sauce

Everybody needs a sauce with some grunt in it, especially to go with some of the rough meals that are cooked over our campfires. This sauce is as tough as an old mallee root.

Ingredients

1 spoon of margarine
1/4 pannikin of vinegar
1/2 pannikin of tomato sauce
2 spoons of lemon concentrate
1 pannikin of water
1 good spoonful of instant coffee powder
1/2 pannikin of Worcestershire sauce
1/2 pannikin of sugar

How to do it

Melt margarine in a pot and add all the other bits. Stir well until the sugar is dissolved. Bring to the boil.

Shift pot to the side of fire if possible and let it just bubble away for 5 minutes or so. Then pour it over the super-beaut meal you've just cooked.

Mushroom Sauce

This is ideal for smothering those hot rissoles you've just cooked.

Ingredients

2 good spoonfuls plain flour
1 pannikin of water
1 crumbed beef stock cube
1 small onion, chopped fine
1 × 190 g can mushrooms

How to do it

In the drained frypan partly cook onions, add flour and stir constantly. Gradually stir in water, stock cube and maintain stirring until mixture boils and thickens. Add mushrooms and stir until mushrooms are heated through.

Serve as *BALLS AND MUSHIES* or on top of any other meal you've got hot, and try it with peas or beans and scones.

Scrub Relish

It's just what you need to give your meat a gentle help-along in the flavour department. No, I don't really mean that, but it helps.

Ingredients

A small amount of jam, preferably plum but anything
A good splash of Worcestershire sauce
A couple of drops of Tabasco sauce
A good slurp of tomato sauce

How to do it

With your fork, and on the side of your plate, mix all the bits together into a paste. It don't look too good mate, but trust me. Then smother your meat with the paste, and enjoy.

Round the Corner

This is the last story of my little book. Hope you enjoyed the read; it has taken over half a century to compile. What a journey it has been; from the highlands in Scotland to the prairies of central Canada, the heat of North Africa to the desolate parts of Australia. I wouldn't have missed it for quids.

This little piece, Round the Corner, explains where I come from and what I'm about. See ya next time.

I come from round the corner down the track along the back
I love to watch the world just pass me by
I hear the little birds whistle their little tunes
And watch the pretty ladies waltz on by

I come from round the corner down the track along the back
I hear the rain it's pounding on my roof
To watch a little dog run up a dusty road
It's great to see the horses on the hoof.

I come from round the corner down the track along the back
I here the wind it's whistling through the trees
To view the sun just setting beneath a bake of clouds
Seeing all that is worth a thousand pounds.

This fellars been around for a while
And seen some changes made
If they ever get it right
It will never ever be the same
I come from round the corner.

Weights And Measures

VOLUME

Imperial	Cup	Metric
1 fluid ounce	1/8 cup	30 ml
2 fl oz	1/4 cup	55 ml
4 fl oz	1/2 cup	115 ml
5 fl oz (1/4 pint)	5/8 cup	140 ml
6 fl oz	3/4 cup	170 ml
8 fl. oz	1 cup	225 ml
10 fl oz (1/2 pint)	1 1/4 cups	285 ml
15 fl oz (3/4 pint)	1 7/8 cups	425 ml
20 fl oz (1 pint)	2 1/2 cups	570 ml

WEIGHT

Imperial	Metric
1 oz	30 g
2 oz	55 g
4 oz (1/4 lb)	115 g
8 oz (1/2 lb)	225 g
12 oz (3/4 lb)	340 g
16 oz (1 lb)	455 g
32 oz (2 lb)	905 g

″ = inch
′ = foot
oz = ounce
lb = pound

LENGTH

Inches	mm	Inches	mm
1	25	7	178
2	51	8	203
3	76	9	229
4	102	10	254
5	127	11	279
6	152	12 (1 foot)	305

THE GEARBOX IS BROKE!!
WELL RING MIDLANDS. THEY HAVE CHANGE OVER GEARBOXES, DIFFS AND ALL THOSE HARD TO GET BITS THAT WILL KEEP YOUR OLD TRUCK GOING
MIDLANDS TRUCK SPARES P/L
319 EAGLEHAWK ROAD
BENDIGO 3556
TEL. 03 5446 8722
FAX.03 5446 1496

NOTES

NOTES

Printed by
McPhersons Printing Group
Maryborough, Victoria.

This book

was knocked together out of a swag
of tasty bits and pieces — deeply embedded in
various computer discs and dubious documents
scraped from the culinary benchtop
of the far-from-ordinary author
Herb (*how'd ya be?*) Lummis.
He's got to be a better cook than he is a speller
— try him on Worcestershire sauce.

All the typographical tidiness here visible
is the work of Shirley Williams, Martin and Christine. And, as usual,
we got the right design nudge at the right time
from our mates, Jimmy and William Britten.

The illustrations flowed from the fine fingers
of the vegetarian illustrator, Debra Hill,
while the editorial challenge
of bringing out the best of *Lummo*
was the work of Christine Flynn and Des Carroll.